# The Manifold Grace of God

As It Relates to Various
Bible Doctrines

Illustrated by the
Parable of the Prodigal Son

**Marvin Penner, Th.M.**

Second Printing


Published by
DreamMaker Press
Denver, Colorado

# Table of Contents

# Preface

This book started out many years ago as a series of sermons on the Manifold Grace of God. After teaching about the grace of God for a number of years, I came to the realization that most of the things I had learned about the grace of God, Jesus taught in one short story; namely, the Parable of the Prodigal Son. I began to wonder if perhaps I was making my study of the grace of God too complicated. Since then, I have always presented the grace of God in the context of this parable.

In presenting the various aspects of God's grace, I came to realize that by doing this I was explaining many areas of theology. Therefore, this book has become a theology book with the doctrine of grace as the outline and the Parable of the Prodigal Son as the illustration. I believe that it could be a great aid in understanding Biblical theology.

This book has been produced with my grandchildren in mind. My desire is that you become godly men and women. I may not be able to contribute much as far as your dedication and devotion to God is concerned, but I am trying to contribute to your knowledge of theology and your understanding of the Bible.

Maybe the mention of theology has you thinking, "This will be boring, theology is for pastors and teachers." Theology is simply knowing and understanding God. What could be more important and exciting than knowing the One who not only designed and created the universe, but also gave each of us life and has a plan for our lives?

July 13, 2010

# A Prayer

This effort is hereby dedicated to God. Whether in study, meditation, writing, or rewriting, it is done as unto the Lord. Whether good or bad, long or short, complete or incomplete, it shall be a labor of love, an expression of dedication, an act of worship. May its reading also be consecrated to God so that no one shall read but that the Holy Spirit move in the heart and mind of the reader.

The Author

## About the Author

Marvin Penner graduated from Grace Bible Institute (now Grace University) with a bachelor's degree in Bible, and earned a Master of Theology degree from Grace Theological Seminary with a major in New Testament and Greek. He has served as pastor of several churches in Minnesota and Montana and has taught at the Evangelical Theological College in Addis Ababa, Ethiopia. He has also been on the staff of several Christian organizations. He and his wife, Sue, live in Williston, North Dakota. They have three children and eleven grandchildren.

If you have any comments or questions about the contents of this book you may call or write.

909 8th Ave. W.
Williston, ND 58801
701-774-8100

# The Story of the Prodigal Son

He was an unusual father. No one knew the extent of his resources, but everyone could see that he was extremely generous. The hired help was well paid, and the family was well provided for. The family consisted of two boys—young men, that is.

The two sons were very different in personality and character, and the wise father, recognizing this, treated them in ways appropriate for their personality.

The younger son was outgoing, fun-loving and liked to do things his own way. He took advantage of his father's generosity and asked for anything he wanted, and the father kept giving. However, with the giving came instructions and warnings because the father did not want his son to encounter difficult or harmful situations as a result of his generosity. Since this son was a self-willed person, he rebelled against the instructions and warnings of his father.

Knowing the father was always generous, this youngest son dared to make a bold request. He asked that his share of the inheritance be given to him now. The father had determined to be generous in everything he did, so he gave his son what he asked for. This son was not content with having his share of the father's wealth at his disposal. He wanted not even the nearness of the father to remind him to do what he ought rather than what he wanted, so he soon packed up everything and left home to live it up in a *far country.*

While his father's bounty lasted, the *far country* was a pleasant experience with many things to see and do and with many friends. However, eventually the funds were depleted and at the same time the *far country* was experiencing a famine. The wayward son, being hungry, got a job herding hogs. Even so, he continued to be hungry. The *far country* was not even able to meet the needs of its citizens, much less satisfy one who knew about the abundance in the father's house.

Now he had time and motive to think about his life and to see clearly where he had gone wrong. He remembered the bounty he had experienced in his father's house. He thought about his present condition and how it compared to the generosity in the father's house. Being humbled in the pigpen, the young man made a wise decision. He did an about-face and decided to go back to his father and confess his sin and humbly ask for the generosity of the father. Now, instead of demanding the father's generosity, he realized that he needed to be like a servant and humbly admit that he was in need of it.

The father saw him coming when he was still a long way off and ran to meet him. He welcomed his son home with hugs and kisses. He gave him special gifts: clothes (not work clothes but dress clothes), shoes and a ring. The father was so full of joy that he acted as if his son had come back from the dead. He wanted everyone to rejoice over the return of his son so he threw a big party with a lot of food, music and dancing.

Now the other son, the older, is also part of the story. While his brother was out wasting the family fortune, he was faithfully working for the father. Outwardly, he was doing all that the father required, but inwardly he was in rebellion toward his father. This son could not see eye to eye with his father because they totally disagreed on one thing—the importance of generosity. The father considered generosity to be a great virtue. The son had no appreciation of generosity. He had never had a party such as was given for his brother because he was so stingy that he could not think of anyone with whom he would want to share some of his father's bounty

Since the older brother did not approve of generosity, he was very upset with his father for being so generous toward his wayward brother. Therefore, he stayed out in the field refusing to join in with the celebration over his brother's return.

The father went out to urge his oldest son to come in and join the celebration. He reminded his son that the entire estate was his. He explained that the safe return of a wayward son was more than enough reason to be generous and to celebrate with a big party.

The story ends with the father out pleading with this son who seemed to have a good relationship with him. However, inwardly the son rebelled against the father because he did not understand or accept the generosity of the father.

# Introduction
# Grace Illustrated

The Parable of the Prodigal Son is not primarily about the prodigal, although it is named after him. Nor is it about the older brother, although he represents the Pharisees to whom Jesus spoke the parable. The parable is all about the unusual generosity of the father. This generosity represents the grace of God. Grace in everyday language is generosity.

Studying the Parable of the Prodigal Son with the various aspects of the grace of God in mind clarifies details of the parable that otherwise are puzzling. Some of the questions that are answered are these:

1. Why did the prodigal have the audacity to ask for his portion of the inheritance?

2. Why did the father give away the inheritance?

3. Why did the prodigal go to a *far country?*

4. Why was the prodigal unable to provide for himself in the *far country?*

5. Why did the famine so drastically affect the prodigal?

6. Why did the prodigal offer himself to his father as a servant?

7. Why was the prodigal given a robe, shoes and a ring?

8. Why did the father insist on a time of celebration?

9. Why does the story involve two sons who are so different from each other?

10. Why was the older son displeased with the father?

11. Why did the older son never have a celebration?

12. Why does the story end with the older brother still out in the field?

Many sermons have been preached and many books written about the grace of God. Nevertheless, there is an area of study that needs greater emphasis. Ephesians 3:2 uses the phrase "the dispensation of the grace of God." What is this referring to? What is a dispensation? Evidently, there is a dispensation that involves grace and there are other dispensations in which grace does not play as prominent a part.

This book presents the various aspects of grace from a dispensational perspective; therefore, an appendix is included which gives a more complete explanation of what we mean by *dispensation.*

# One
# The Grace of God

*Then He said: "A certain man had two sons. And the younger of them said unto his father. 'Father, give me that portion of goods that falls to me. He divided to them his livelihood. And not many days after, the younger son gathered all together, journeyed to a far country, and there wasted his possessions with prodigal living."* Luke 15:11

Several of the parables of Jesus are characterized by the fact that they are true to life except in one detail, and in that detail is the main point of the parable. In this parable, the main lesson is in the unusual generosity of the father, for it depicts to us the grace of God.

We call this story the Parable of the Prodigal Son, however, the story is not primarily about the younger son who went astray and came back. Nor is it about the older son pouting in the field. The parable is about the astounding generosity of the father. First, "he divided to them his livelihood." Then he welcomed back, with lavish gifts, the son who squandered his possessions. The father told the older son, "All that I have is yours." This generosity is one of the best illustrations of the grace of God. The way this father treated his sons is the way God treats us—not all the same, but all fairly and with generosity.

The father in the parable divided his livelihood between his sons. This is the first act of generosity mentioned in the story.

It was a very generous act, and it sets the pattern for the rest of the story, because there are other generous acts that follow. Each one was an expression of the father's character. It was not the insistence of the sons that motivated this generosity. Nor did the father do what he did because he considered his sons worthy of it. In every situation, he was true to his character and faithful to act in accordance with the kind of father he had determined to be. Likewise, the grace of God is an expression of God's character. God is love and out of this love comes the generosity that we call the grace of God (1 John 4:7-9). Before time existed, God loved.

God is three in one. We understand God to be one—one being, one essence, one God. However, there is something about God that is three. We call it three persons, God the Father, God the Son and God the Holy Spirit. Each does what persons do: speak, feel, love, etc.

God has existed as three persons throughout all of eternity past. Since He is one God in three persons, He could and did experience love. God the Father loved God the Son and the Son loved the Father (John 17). Therefore, the joys of loving and being loved have always existed. However, God's capacity to love was larger than this, so He created a world to love. This is the basis of the grace of God.

*For God so loved the World that He gave his one and only begotten Son, that whoever believes in Him should not perish but have everlasting life.* John 3:16

# Two
# Grace and the Character of God

*A certain man had two sons. He divided to them his livelihood.*
Luke 15:11-12

The father in the story of the Prodigal Son had one outstanding quality, he was generous. But notice, he was not extravagant. That is, his generosity was not designed to be wasteful, purposeless or selfish. His generosity came from his goodness. All that he did, especially in his generosity, was designed to benefit his sons.

Our Heavenly Father is a good God. We must understand God's goodness; otherwise we do not have a God, but a demon or worse.

Let me illustrate it this way. The God of the Bible created and controls the world. To do this, He must possess certain qualities. Suppose when we get to heaven one of our assigned responsibilities is to create our own world to take care of. Suppose God says, "First make a shopping list of everything that you will need." I know what I would put on my list. I would only need to list two items. However, if I were given the responsibility to check your list to see if you had everything that is required, I would insist that you have a third item that I would not necessarily feel I needed for myself. That may sound strange but let us think it through. The only way I could create a world would be if I had infinite wisdom and infinite power. In other words, I would have to know everything there is to know and have the power to do anything I decide to do. Therefore, those are the two items on my list.

That is the kind of God we have and that is what it took to create the world. However, if you had that kind of power, I would be afraid because I do not know what you would do with all that power. Would you be a mean and cruel master over your world? Or more to the point, what would you do to me? If you were to have infinite power and wisdom, it would be most important to me that you also have qualities such as goodness, kindness, love and mercy. Fortunately, the God of creation is also a loving Heavenly Father who loves what He has created. Out of this love for the world comes the marvelous grace of God. This love is not just a sentimental kind of love but a love that cost something, as we will see in the following chapters.

*The grace of the Lord Jesus Christ, and the love of God, and the communion of the Holy Spirit be with you all. Amen.*
2 Corinthians 13:14

# Three
# Grace Involves Freedom

*Then He said: "A certain man had two sons. And the younger of them said unto his father, 'Father, give me that portion of goods that falls to me.' He divided to them his livelihood. And not many days after, the younger son gathered all together, journeyed to a far country, and there wasted his possessions with prodigal living."* Luke 15:11-12

This father knew that if he really loved his sons, he would have to let them make their own choices and experience some of the consequences. He let the younger son leave even though he knew the potential of evil that lay ahead.

Likewise, the Heavenly Father knew that in order to give and receive the full expression of love, there had to be freedom. We call this man's *free will*. With freedom comes the possibility of rebellion. Nonetheless, as it relates to free will, God created three kinds of beings. One kind is incapable of making moral decisions. They have no need or opportunity to choose how to relate to their Maker. These are the animals. They do not have freedom to change what they are, for they live by instinct. They cannot love and be loved like God loves or like humans can.

Another kind of being God created had the opportunity to make a choice of submitting to God's will or rebelling against their Maker. These are the angels. Some of them did rebel and followed Satan.

The third kind of being is mankind. Man was created with a free will. He had the opportunity to choose to submit to God's will or to rebel. He chose to disobey God and his sin alienated him from God. But now the love of God could provide a way for forgiveness to be possible. Sin has a penalty. There is a price that has to be paid. For the angels who sinned, there was no one who could act on their behalf and pay the price. However, since man was made in the image of God, God Himself could represent mankind and pay the penalty on man's behalf. He did this by becoming a man. The second person of the Trinity took on humanity by coming to earth as a baby. The result was that Jesus, Son of God and son of man, is fully God and fully man. This is what grace is all about. This is what allows God to be generous on man's behalf. The resources of the infinite God are made available to man's side of the ledger so that man might be forgiven and restored to fellowship with God.

It is the grace of God that truly sets men free, because true freedom is not only in being free to run away but in also being free to come back. The prodigal thought he would find freedom in the *far country*. Instead, he found bondage. Back home, in the father's arms, that was where he became free—free from guilt, from domination, from loss, from want.

*But we see Jesus, who was made a little lower than the angels, for the suffering of death crowned with glory and honor, that He, by the grace of God, might taste death for everyone.* Hebrews 2:9

*But now having been set free from sin, and having become slaves of God, you have your fruit to holiness, and the end, everlasting life. For the wages of sin is death, but the gift of God is eternal life in Christ Jesus our Lord.* Romans 6:22–23

# Four
# Common Grace

*And the younger of them said to his father, "Father, give me the portion of goods that falls to me." So he divided to them his livelihood.* Luke 15:12

*But when he had spent all . . . he began to be in want.* Luke 15:14

The father was so generous in all his dealings that the younger son made a bold request. He asked that his share of the inheritance be given to him now. The father, true to his character, gave him what he asked for.

This represents the aspect of God's grace that is called common grace. Common grace is God's blessings in the physical realm. It involves the creation of the world, for this world was created for man's benefit. "[God] gives us richly all things to enjoy" (1 Timothy 6:17).

Common grace was first given when Adam and Eve were placed in the Garden of Eden. There, mankind had a perfect environment. Everything that Adam and Eve could need was abundantly supplied. However, Adam and Eve, like the prodigal, were not content with the abundance provided for them. They, too, refused to live under the control of the One who provided everything for them.

Common grace is sometimes called *damning grace* because it does not provide salvation. It is given to the saved and the unsaved alike. "For He makes His sun rise on the evil and on the good, and sends rain on the just and on the unjust" (Matthew 5:45). We all respond to common grace in much the same way as the prodigal did and the way Adam and Eve did. When we, early in life, begin to see all the potential in what the world can provide in terms of things, pleasures, experiences, relationships and security, we all determine to get for ourselves all that we can. Like the prodigal, we feel that it is due us, and we take all we can with no thought of owing submission and gratitude to the God who provided them.

Like the bounty that the prodigal received from his father, common grace allows us to enjoy the things of this world and even "the passing pleasures of sin" (Hebrews 11:25). However, like the prodigal, eventually we realize that common grace is not enough—we come up short financially, or we lose our health. Finally, in old age, we realize that we are spiritually bankrupt and have nothing provided for eternity.

Mankind's great need is for saving grace. Common grace fulfills its purpose when it turns us to God to receive the saving grace we so desperately need.

*Or do you despise the riches of His goodness, forbearance, and long-suffering, not knowing that the goodness of God leads you to repentance?* Romans 2:4

# Five
# The Cost of Grace—
# a Substitutionary Sacrifice

*And the younger of them said to his father, "Father, give me the portion of goods that falls to me." So he divided to them his livelihood.* Luke 15:12

The father, in order to be true to his own self-determined quality of generosity, gave the younger son what he asked for. Evidently, in order to be totally fair, he gave his older son his share as well, for the Scripture says, "So he divided to them his livelihood." This act of generosity cost the father everything.

The grace of God is a free gift to the recipient, but God paid a tremendous price to make it available. To provide for the physical needs of His creatures was easy. To provide for the spiritual needs (not just forgiveness and restoration to fellowship but new life to those who are spiritually dead) required an infinite supply of love. To make possible the expression of this love, God planned, from the beginning, for provision to be made so that He could forgive those who do wrong. This provision was made by sending His Son to earth to give His life as a substitutionary sacrifice.

God gave freely and generously until there was nothing else to give, so that He could provide not merely material blessings, which last only a short time, but spiritual blessings, which last forever. This includes forgiveness and new life

(Colossians 2:11‑14), a new relationship with the Father (Ephesians 2:18‑19), the guaranteed seal of the Holy Spirit (2 Corinthians 1:22), assurance of eternal life (John 3:36), and a share in the inheritance of Jesus Christ (Colossians 3:24).

All this is for anyone who will receive it by faith alone, for the price has been paid. The cost was so great that it is an insult to God for us to think that we can contribute anything toward the cost. This high price He was willing to pay.

*For you know the grace of our Lord Jesus Christ, that though He was rich, yet for your sakes He became poor, that you through His poverty might become rich.* 2 Corinthians 8:9

# Six
# The Cost of Grace—Forbearance

*And not many days after, the younger son gathered all together, journeyed to a far country, and there wasted his possessions with prodigal living.* Luke 15:13

The generosity of the father cost him more than just his material possessions. He acted with full knowledge of what would happen as a result of his generosity—how it would be misused and the results of that misuse. Therefore, it cost him both the pain of knowing that the possessions intended for the son's perpetual good would be squandered and wasted and the pain of knowing that eventually the son would end up in dire circumstances. These are the hidden costs of generosity, hidden from others but felt deeply by the one who loves enough to be generous.

The grace of God also has a hidden cost. It is the cost of forbearance. By this we mean that God was willing to endure the existence of sin and to delay judging sin in order to put into effect His plan of salvation and to give individuals opportunity and time to repent and turn to Him (Romans 9:22–23). It was the grace of God that made Him willing to let men have freedom to choose and then to withhold judgment until a substitutionary sacrifice was made.

God's forbearance can be seen most clearly during certain times in history. From Adam to Noah, God acted in forbearance. Individuals were allowed to live as they pleased without immediate judgment from God. Even Cain, who killed his brother, was allowed to live out his life in peace. From Abraham to the Exodus, God acted with forbearance in that God chose to deal with one individual and one family and let the rest of the world go their own way while judgment was withheld.

The same forbearance is in effect today during this Dispensation of Grace. God does not give out immediate judgment on sinners. Seldom do we see any connection between a person's sin and his prosperity. This does not mean that sin will go unpunished. Judgment is merely delayed.

In Noah's day, the flood came suddenly and destroyed all of the sinners. In Egypt, the ten plagues were God's judgment. The cup of the iniquities of the Amorites was not full when Abraham lived in the land (Genesis 15:16). He left them to their evil practices, but Joshua was commanded to destroy them because the time of forbearance had ended and the time of judgment had come (Deuteronomy 20:17).

Likewise, in the near future God's forbearance will end and the time of judgment described in Revelation chapters 6 through 19 will come to pass. "Truly, these times of ignorance God overlooked, but now commands all men everywhere to repent" (Acts 17:30).

God is always a God of grace, but during these times of forbearance, His grace is most evident. Thank God, we live in a time of forbearance when He gives time and opportunity to repent and to experience His saving grace.

*Being justified freely by His grace through the redemption that is in Christ Jesus, whom God set forth as a propitiation by His blood, through faith. . , to demonstrate at the present time His righteousness, that He might be just and the justifier of the one who has faith in Jesus.* Romans 3:24-26

# Seven
# The Grace of Our Lord Jesus Christ—
# Propitiation

*So he divided to them his livelihood. Bring out the best robe and put it on him, and put a ring on his hand and sandals on his feet. . . and all that I have is yours.* Luke 15:12,22,31

The prodigal son received the benefits of a generous father whenever he was in the father's presence. This generosity allowed him freedom to make choices, to go his own way, to experience what the *far country* had to offer, both the good and the bad. Most importantly, it allowed him to come back to the father and enjoy his generosity continuously. This father always acted with generosity and it was always at his own expense. We wonder how he could continually have the resources to be so generous.

The grace of God is available at God's expense, and there is always an abundant resource. However, grace is only possible because of what was provided through the Lord Jesus Christ. His death on the cross provides an infinite source of grace, for it was an infinite sacrifice.

God cannot act graciously just because He is loving and good. A way has to be provided, a means by which He can act graciously. It is a little bit like owing someone money. That person may say, "I forgive this debt." But that is not enough. There is a price to be paid. Someone has to stand the loss. In theological terms this is called *propitiation.* It involves a price that was paid to clear our slate, as it were, so that we can be right with God.

Propitiation is needed because what makes sin sinful is that it produces bad consequences, and someone has to bear those consequences. Furthermore, the holiness of God requires that all evil receive appropriate recompense. God cannot act graciously apart from the person and work of Jesus Christ. Christ, and Christ alone, provides what is necessary for God to act toward us in grace. The only reason the individuals in the Old Testament could experience the grace of God was that, in the mind of God, Christ and His cross experience were already established facts (see Romans 3:24‒26). John 1:17 says, "Grace and truth came through Jesus Christ."

Grace is impossible apart from Jesus Christ. However, we can take that a step further—because of Jesus Christ, God must act in grace. The means has been provided. The price has been paid. The supply line has been laid. The reservoir is full. What Jesus supplied was infinite—no limit and no end. Anyone coming to God in the name of Jesus must receive the grace of God. That is a sure guarantee.

*But now having been set free from sin, and having become slaves of God, you have your fruit to holiness, and the end, everlasting life. For the wages of sin is death, but the gift of God is eternal life in Christ Jesus our Lord.* Romans 6:22‒23

*For if by the one man's offense death reigned through the one, much more those who receive abundance of grace and of the gift of righteousness will reign in life through the One, Jesus Christ. Therefore, as through one man's offense judgment came to all men, resulting in condemnation, even so through one Man's righteous act the free gift came to all men, resulting in justification of life.* Romans 5:17-18

# Eight
# Grace Is Restrictive—It Sets Up Limits

*And not many days after, the younger son gathered all together, journeyed to a far country, and there wasted his possessions with prodigal living.* Luke 15:13

Why did the prodigal go to a *far country* instead of staying in familiar territory? Evidently, he wanted to be totally free from the control of his father. He knew that what he wanted to do did not please his father. The father's love, if it were allowed to determine his actions, would put severe restrictions on his lifestyle. He knew that if he stayed near home, just the nearness of his father would remind him of those restrictions and this he did not want. So, to escape the restrictions that the mere presence of the father imposed upon him, he put as much distance between his father and himself as he could.

The grace of God is restrictive—it sets up limits. God's love and generosity supply that which is for our greatest good. Therefore, God's grace requires that our activities also be in line with that which is good for us.

Adam and Eve, in the perfect environment of the Garden of Eden, were restricted by the command not to eat of the Tree of the Knowledge of Good and Evil. Eating the fruit of that tree brought death. This is called the *fall of man.*

The fall had results that are still obvious today. It brought about separation from God, which is death. God said, "In the day that you eat of it you shall surely die (Genesis 2:17)." Therefore, as soon as Adam sinned by eating the forbidden fruit, his body began a deterioration that resulted in physical death. Moreover, he passed on to his descendants a fallen sin nature that involves spiritual death, which is separation from God.

Do we ask God to be generous to us when we are not willing to spend time in His presence, lest our deeds be reproved? Grace from God is provided not so that we can have the things we want the most, but so that we can have what is best for us. The more we understand the importance of grace in our lives, the more we are moved to do what is right. However, if we are not interested in God's will for our lives, He will let us go our own way—away from His grace. The grace of God is available to all but not experienced by all.

*God resists the proud, but gives grace to the humble. . . . Therefore, humble yourselves under the mighty hand of God, that He may exalt you in due time.* 1 Peter 5:5‒6

# Nine

# Grace Is Exclusive—It Lets the Rebellious Go Their Own Way

*And not many days after, the younger son gathered all together, journeyed to a far country, and there wasted his possessions with prodigal living.* Luke 15:13

The prodigal was allowed to do what he wanted to do and go where he wanted to go. Since his mind was made up, the father made no effort to stop him. It was best for him to leave for several reasons. If he stayed home, it would only have led to more rebellion. Furthermore, there were lessons to be learned that are best learned in the *far country.* Therefore, the generosity of the father allowed the son to leave home even though this generosity was available and adequate only in the father's house.

God sent mankind into the *far country* when He dealt with the descendants of Noah at the Tower of Babel (Genesis 11). He did this by confusing their language. The reason He scattered them over the whole world was to restrain their rebellion in everything they imagined to do.

After he wasted all his possessions in the *far country,* the prodigal began to lack the necessities of life. The *far country* could not meet his needs, for it could not even meet the needs of its own citizens. The generosity of the father was not available in the *far country.* There was no thought of asking his father for assistance. He did not, as in the old story of the college student who needed more money, telegraph home saying, "No mon, no fun, your son"; for he too would have expected to hear back, "Too bad, so sad, your dad."

He never called home and said, "The economy here is in bad shape; you have a lot of influence, can't you do something about it?" He never wrote and said, "I need a job. Can you get someone here to hire me?"

Yet some whose lives show that they are far from the Heavenly Father's heart call upon God in a time of need to provide what they desire for their own pleasure and comfort, even though they are not interested in a relationship with Him.

The bounty of the father seemed to be well suited for life in the *far country*, but in reality, it proved to be ineffective in maintaining the lifestyle of the *far country*. The enduring aspects of the father's provision were available only to those in his presence.

The grace of God is always available; however, we must not presume upon the grace of God. Certain qualifications have to be met. God's grace is not provided so that we can more fully enjoy the pleasures of this life, rather its purpose is primarily to provide for our eternal well−being. It is those whose lives are centered on the Father's eternal home who experience the grace of God. First, go home to the Father and be reconciled to God by believing in His Son, then all the eternal treasures of His grace will become available.

*Therefore, having been justified by faith, we have peace with God through our Lord Jesus Christ through whom also we have access by faith into this grace, in which we stand, and rejoice in hope of the glory of God.* Romans 5:1-2

# Ten
# Where Grace Is Unavailable

*But when he had spent all, there arose a severe famine in that land and he began to be in want. Then he went and joined himself to a citizen of that country, and he sent him into his fields to feed swine.* Luke 15:14-15

Plenty of money, plenty of food, plenty of friends, many things to see and do—this was the *far country.* It seemed grand, but it did not last. Father's fortune was spent and no more was available in the *far country.*

Ever since Adam and Eve sinned, man has lived in a *far country.* The bounties of God's creation and man's capability to enjoy them make for an enticing combination. Thus, man has become involved with many activities and pursuits. God has given man freedom to choose; and man, for the most part, has chosen to leave Him out of the picture. Taking God into account would involve being responsible to Him for one's actions.

People choose the *far country* lifestyle and eventually find their lives to be a famine. They hear about God's grace, about how generous God is and about His promises to meet their needs. So they ask God to give them what they want. When God does not give them what they ask for, they discredit the Word of God, the promises of God and the grace of God. They are hoping to enjoy the generosity of the Father and still remain in the *far country.*

We must realize that God's grace is not available in the *far country*. We cannot rebel against the will of God and at the same time expect to experience His grace. So you see, the grace of God is restrictive—it sets limits. Furthermore, the grace of God is exclusive—it lets rebels go their own way. It is available to all, but not all receive it.

Do we ask God to be generous to us when we are not willing to spend time in His presence lest our deeds be reproved? Grace from God is provided not so that we can have the things we want the most, but so that we can have what is best for us. The more we understand the importance of grace in our lives, the more we are moved to do what is right. However, if we are not interested in God's will for our lives, He will let us go our own way, away from His grace. The grace of God is available to all but not experienced by all.

Living in the *far country* had a good result because it turned the prodigal around. So also, God allows us to have pigpen experiences. Being destitute and feeding swine produced the humility he needed to go back to his father with the right attitude. Just as the *far country* could not meet the prodigal's long-term needs, so this world cannot provide for our eternal life. All that material things can do is remind us of a generous God so that we will turn to Him and get what we really need.

*But God be thanked* [literal translation *"Grace to God"*] *that though you were slaves of sin, yet you obeyed from the heart that form of doctrine to which you were delivered. And having been set free from sin, you became slaves of righteousness.* Romans 6:17‒18

# Eleven
# Grace and the Authority of Government

*Then he went and joined himself to a citizen of that country, and he sent him into his fields to feed swine.* Luke 15:15

The prodigal son, at first, did not intend to become attached to the *far country*. He was merely a tourist enjoying the sights, experiences, merchandise and companionship it had to offer. He had no connection to the *far country*, no citizenship, no civil responsibility. He was going to do his own thing, rely on the provisions of the father's house and let the country take care of its own affairs.

He found out that it did not work that way. If you live in a *far country*, you have obligations to the country you live in even if it is far from perfect in its resources. Everything changed when he realized that all of his resources had been wasted and he began to be hungry. He looked to the *far country* to meet his needs. "Then he went and joined himself to a citizen of that country . . ." (Luke 15:15). Now he had an identity in that country, he came under its jurisdiction. He received benefits from it and had responsibilities to it.

The prodigal's relationship to the *far country* can be used to illustrate our relationship to the world we live in and the country we live in. The generosity of our heavenly Father, when we turn to Him with repentance and humility, delivers us out of the dominion of this evil age (see chapter thirteen) but temporarily leaves us under the jurisdiction of the country we live in, with certain responsibilities to that country.

Eventually we discover that there is a famine in the land. The resources of our country are far from adequate, especially in regards to eternal things. The military might is incapable of establishing peace in the world. The legal system of our country is far from adequate, especially in its ability to produce godly living. These things only the grace of God can supply. Nonetheless, we do enjoy benefits that come with living in the country we live in, so we have a responsibility to that country.

God established the principle of government, and all governmental authority comes from Him and is an extension of His authority. That is why the Scripture says in Romans 13:1-2:

> For there is no authority except from God, and the authorities that exist are appointed by God. Therefore, whoever resists the authority resists the ordinance of God, and those who resist will bring judgment on themselves.

1 Peter 2:13-14 also speaks along this line.

> Therefore, submit yourselves to every ordinance of man for the Lord's sake, whether to the king as supreme, or to governors, as to those who are sent by him for the punishment of evil doers and for the praise of those who do good.

How and when did God appoint these authorities? It happened in Genesis chapter nine when God established the principle of capital punishment and thereby established human government.

A Christian's responsibility is, first of all, to be in submission. It is clear from Romans 13 that we should submit. We should obey the laws. We should pay taxes. We should show the respect that is expected.

Second, Christians should pray for those who are in positions of authority. 1 Timothy 2:1-2 says that we should pray for kings and for all those who are in authority over us.

Third, Christians should remember that they are also under a higher law—the law of the indwelling Holy Spirit. Grace has put us under this law, which not only commands, but also motivates and enables. This law of the Spirit is not burdensome, for it is a law of freedom. "For the law of the Spirit of life in Christ Jesus has made me free from the law of sin and death" (Romans 8:2). When the command of human government is definitely contrary to the clear command of God, the Christian should obey God rather than man (Acts 4:18-20) and suffer any consequences.

*So that as sin reigned in death, even so grace might reign through righteousness to eternal life through Jesus Christ our Lord.* Romans 5:21

# Twelve
# Grace and the Limitations of Government

*When he had spent all, there was a severe famine in that land, and he began to be in want. Then he went and joined himself to a citizen of that country, and he sent him into his fields to feed swine. And he would gladly have filled his stomach with the pods that the swine ate,* and no one gave him anything. Luke 15:14-16

The *far country* was far because it was a great distance from the heart and desire of the father. It was a country because it had its own national and political identity. The father's authority was not recognized there, so when provisions were depleted, the prodigal was forced to become a part of the local economy, even though that economy was so bad that people were starving. However, the prodigal also had another, higher authority. He belonged in his father's house, under the father's jurisdiction.

What does the country we live in have to do with our understanding of the grace of God? The Dispensation (Administration) of the Grace of God (Ephesians 3:2) refers to how God works and rules in the hearts of men and/or in the affairs of nations. Grace, in this context, stands in contrast to the Old Testament laws and to the authority of human government. Therefore, to understand the Dispensation of Grace we need to understand how it contrasts with the Dispensation of Government.

The Dispensation of Grace means that believers receive, as a free gift, power and wisdom to live a godly life. This work of the Holy Spirit also produces in the Christian a gracious lifestyle. This lifestyle is described in detail in the Sermon on the Mount (Matthew 5-7). Go the second mile, turn the other cheek, give to whoever asks, love your enemies—these are a few of the commands. Some might say this is not for today, it will not work. No, it will not work for unbelievers. But it worked for Jesus and it works for His followers.

Here is the part that may be misunderstood. There are two administrations going on at the same time. We get ourselves into theological trouble if we try to put everyone under the Administration of Grace. Everyone has grace available to him and can be saved by grace. However, not everyone is living under grace, only those who have been saved by grace. Those who are not saved by grace are not subject to the Administration of Grace. "Because the carnal mind is enmity against God; for it is not subject to the law of God, nor indeed can be" (Romans 8:7). So you see, Christians are under an administration that the rest of the world is not subject to. This helps us determine the rights and responsibilities of government and the responsibility of a Christian to the government.

The government has every right to exercise its authority. It can even go to the extent of capital punishment; or maybe we should say it has to go to the extent of capital punishment if it is to maintain the kind of control that it should maintain. This authority is mentioned in Romans 13:3-4:

> For the rulers are not a terror to good works, but to evil. Do you want to be unafraid of the authority? Do good and you will have praise from the same. For he is God's minister to you for good. But if you do evil, be afraid,

for he does not bear the sword in vain; for he is God's minister, an avenger to execute wrath on him who practices evil.

For the present, the instruction given in the Sermon on the Mount will not work for governments. There are those who say the military is wrong, we should do away with it. This truly is the ideal and would be fine and good if everyone were under grace; and, of course, in the future administration this will be the case. For the present, the government has the right to maintain and use its army. We have to allow government to function in the only way it can function. However, we as Christians do not function that way. Under the Administration of Grace, we not only receive grace, we extend grace. So living by the principles taught in the Sermon on the Mount is a part of living under grace. Go the second mile, turn the other cheek, give to whoever asks, and love your enemies. Take time to read Matthew 5–7 and see what living under grace involves.

*And God is able to make all grace abound toward you, that you, always having all sufficiency in all things, may have an abundance for every good work.* 2 Corinthians 9:8

# Thirteen
# Grace and This Present Evil Age

*But when he came to himself, he said, ". . . I will arise and go to my father."* Luke 15:17–18

The father's house and the *far country* stand in stark contrast. In the father's house, there is generosity. In the *far country*, there is want and hunger. The prodigal not only had to go to the father's house, but he also had to leave the *far country* and all the attractive but temporary things it had to offer.

Being in a *far country* produced in the prodigal the realization that he had made bad choices and that some changes needed to be made. However, it also meant that he needed to do more than change his mind, more than speak the appropriate words. He was in the wrong location. He was not in the right domain. He needed to get up and go. He needed to be under the jurisdiction of his father, not of the *far country*.

To understand fully the grace of God and its benefits we must know about the *far country* that we all have chosen to live in, the *far country* that we need to leave if we are to enjoy the generosity of God's saving grace. This *far country* can represent the age we are living in. As a result of Adam's sin in the Garden of Eden and our own personal sins, we all find ourselves in the *far country*. Therefore, we experience some of the same things the prodigal experienced and we have to have a similar change of mind and heart.

The way that the prodigal related to his generous father while in the *far country* illustrates for us the condition we were in before we experienced the saving grace of God.

The word *age* in the Bible refers to the world system. It is the world apart from and in opposition to God. It has much to offer, it has its allurement, but it is all temporary.

Notice how the Bible describes the age in which we live. "Grace to you and peace from God the Father and our Lord Jesus Christ, who gave Himself for our sins, that He might deliver us from this present evil age, according to the will of our God and Father. To whom be glory forever and ever. Amen" (Galatians 1:35). The Bible calls the age in which we are living "this present evil age." Therefore, we might say that when the Bible speaks of the present administration (The Dispensation of the Grace of God, Ephesians 3:2), it refers to God's workings—to grace. However, when the Bible speaks of "this age," it has to do with Satan's working. 2 Corinthians 4:3-4 refers to this.

"But even if our gospel is veiled, it is veiled to those who are perishing, whose minds the god of this age has blinded, who do not believe, lest the light of the gospel of the glory of Christ, who is the image of God, should shine on them."

Thus we see that this age has as its god the one who blinds people to the light of the gospel—that is Satan himself.

How does the Christian relate to this age? We note, first, that this age relates most directly to the Christian's past. Ephesians 2:1-2 makes this clear.

And He made you alive, who were dead in the trespasses and sins in which you formerly walked according to the age of this world, according to the prince of the authority of the air, that is the spirit that is now working in the sons of disobedience (author's translation).

So, our past was according to this present age. Before we came into a right relationship with God through faith in His Son, the realm of our existence and activity was this present age.

Romans 12:2 refers to this. "And stop being conformed to this present age but be transformed by the renewing of your mind" (author's translation).

The problem included our mind–set. We tend to think in terms of this world which has only a temporary existence. If we are to enjoy eternal life, a change is needed. This is where God's grace enters the picture. Our part in this change is called repentance—a change of mind, a turning around to go in the opposite direction. God's part is called conversion—change on the inside.

Notice that these passages do not leave us in a relationship with the present age. Romans chapter 12 talks about a transformation. This is what God's grace does. Ephesians 2:6 also goes on to show us what happens when God's grace enters the picture. "[God] raised us up together, and made us sit together in the heavenly places in Christ Jesus." It is like being transferred out of one age into another. We are now living in relation to the coming age rather than the present age. Colossians 1:13 says: "He has delivered us from the power of darkness and conveyed us into the kingdom of the Son of His love."

Maybe we as Christians should make more of the difference between the past and the present. Does the person who sits next to you in church have a sordid past? That can be expected. He used to be a part of this present evil age. We all did. What is our life like now? There should be a change from what we used to be.

*Grace to you and peace from God the Father and our Lord Jesus Christ, who gave Himself for our sins, that He might deliver us from this present evil age, according to the will of our God and Father, to whom be glory forever and ever. Amen.*
Galatians 1:3‒5

# Fourteen
# Requirements of Grace

*But when he came to himself, he said, "How many of my father's hired servants have bread enough and to spare, and I perish with hunger! I will arise and go to my father, and will say to him, 'Father, I have sinned against heaven and before you, and I am no longer worthy to be called your son. Make me like one of your hired servants.'"* Luke 15:17–19

The next thing the prodigal experienced was, in some ways, the best thing that could have happened to him. He found himself in a pigpen. By getting a job feeding swine he learned things and experienced things that he would have missed otherwise. He became a part of the economy of the *far country* and found it to be totally inadequate in meeting his needs.

One who had never experienced the generosity of the father as he had experienced it might have been content with the swine. For this young man such a menial occupation, that left him hungrier than the swine, was not acceptable, but that experience was what he needed to bring him to his senses.

The generosity of the father did not last in the *far country*, but the memory of it did. Herding the swine, though the chore was unpleasant, was profitable, because it gave him time to think. He thought about his miserable condition and the lifestyle that got him to this point. Moreover, he remembered what it was like in his father's house. In particular, he remembered his father's generosity; how even the lowest paid servants had what they needed and more. If only there was the possibility of again experiencing a bit of his father's generosity.

Fortunately, the prodigal knew what he would have to do in order to have even the hope of experiencing the generosity of his father. He would have to leave where he was and go to where the father was—the reverse of what he had done. The *far country* experiences and relationships would have to be forsaken for good. He would have to go to his father's house, to the place where he first made a wrong decision. There he would have to stand in the presence of his father and face up to his wrong doings.

So it was that the generosity of his father along with the severity of his present condition brought the young man to the place where he was willing to make a total change (Romans 2:4). He changed his way of thinking and his course of action, and the result was something wonderful.

All this teaches us about our relationship to our Heavenly Father. We too must come to the place where we think honestly about our spiritual condition and then remember the grace of God.

Then we have to turn around and go to the Father, which is the opposite direction from the way we have been going, knowing that all we need comes from the Father. This is called repentance.

*But by the grace of God I am what I am, and His grace toward me was not in vain; but I labored more abundantly than they all, yet not I, but the grace of God which was with me.*
1 Corinthians 15:10

# Fifteen
# Grace to the Humble

*Make me like one of your hired servants. I am no longer worthy to be called your son.* Luke 15:19&21

When the prodigal returned home, he was planning to be like a servant in his father's household since he considered himself no longer worthy to be treated as a son. Was this a good plan? The father did not pay much attention to this idea for he had other plans for his son, but the attitude was right. It pleased the father. The pride that was his downfall was gone, replaced by humility, which not only allowed him to go back to his father but also enabled him to say the right words to his father. With a truly humble attitude he could admit his wrong doing to his father and then expect to get what he needed, not because he demanded it but because he knew that the generosity of his father provided it.

Like the prodigal, we have nothing with which to pay for our wrongdoing. God's grace does not require us to pay for our sins; it does not even allow us to try to pay for our sins. However, there are conditions under which grace is available and other conditions under which it is not available. We cannot experience God's saving grace by making demands. Everyone who comes to God must come with humility. Like the prodigal, we must come to the place where we admit the truth of the matter and see ourselves as we really are. God's grace is experienced when we come to Him in humility.

Let us think again about the potential of our lives. Looking at the vast expanse of God's creation, thinking about our unreached goals and dreams, reviewing again the goodness of God shown through common grace, we realize that we cannot be content with what we have experienced in this world. We loathe the failures, the frustrations, and the limitations this life has brought to us. However, it is these very things that produce in us the humility that drives us to the Father, earnestly seeking that throne of grace where we can find what our inner being craves.

Those who would experience the grace of God must, like the prodigal, leave and go. The grace of God is not something we can add, like a supplement, to our own resources, or come to once in a while when we run short on that which the world supplies. If we are to experience the grace of God we must leave our dependence on other things and go to the Father, depending only on His generosity.

*But He gives more grace. Therefore, He says: "God resists the proud, but gives grace to the humble."* James 4:6

# Sixteen
## Grace is Selective—It Chooses

*But when he was still a great way off, his father saw him and had compassion, and ran and fell on his neck and kissed him.* Luke 15:20

When did the father decide whether or not to accept the prodigal into the home and into the family? Was it when he heard his words of repentance? Was it when he saw him way down the road on the horizon? Or, did he have a report from observers in the *far country* so that he could make his decision ahead of time? No, none of the above. The decision was made before the prodigal even left home. In fact, all the generosity the prodigal had experienced was for this very end, to bring him back. So, the father was expecting, waiting for and prepared for his return.

We come to the important topic of election. How does grace relate to the topic of election? How can grace be selective?

Some present the doctrine of election in such a way that man really has no choice in the matter of his eternal salvation, it is completely up to God. In other words, sometimes the father accepts the prodigal back and sometimes he does not. Others say it is simply a matter of foreknowledge. The father ran to meet him because he knew what he was going to say.

Both of these views present far too small a picture of election. The Bible teaches that election is not just foreknowledge but predetermination. All that the father did from the beginning, as it pertained to this young man, was designed to bring about not just his return, his repentance, and his acceptance, but all the future joys which their new relationship made possible. Therefore, election does not mean that when I decided to become a believer, God already had made the decision, more or less arbitrarily, for me. Nor is election merely God knowing ahead of time that I would make that decision. Election involves the fact that God, in eternity past, planned to have an eternal relationship with me (Ephesians 1:4) and began to work out that plan. That plan included what Jesus Christ did for me on the cross (Ephesians 1:7), what the Holy Spirit did for me in my heart and mind, what the Holy Spirit is doing in my life, and everything else that happens to me (Romans 8:28⁻30) and that will happen to me when I enter into His presence (Ephesians 1:5⁻12).

Therefore, election is also a work of God's grace (Romans 11:5). It does not prevent anyone from experiencing God's grace. Today God's calling, God's election, and God's grace are for whoever will come to Him. How good it is to know that election works for us, not against us.

*Even so then, at this present time there is a remnant according to the election of grace. And if by grace, then it is no longer of works; otherwise grace is no longer grace. But if it is of works, it is no longer grace; otherwise work is no longer work.*
Romans 11:5⁻6

*For "whoever calls on the name of the Lord shall be saved."*
Romans 10:13

# Seventeen
# Saving Grace—the Eternal Plan

*And he arose and came to his father. But when he was still a great way off, his father saw him and had compassion, and ran and fell on his neck and kissed him.* Luke 15:20

Meanwhile, back at home, the father watched and waited. He lived for the day when his son would return. Since he was watching for him, he saw him coming when he was still a long way off. How would he greet his erring son? On what terms would he welcome him back? Would he be harsh or forgiving? We know that the father is characterized by generosity. Would he still be generous in this situation? Yes, he was even more generous than ever before. Up to this point, we had seen just the beginning of the generosity of the father, and already it has tested our credulity.

The erring son was still a long way off but his father saw him coming, ran to meet him, hugged him, and kissed him. He heard the confession, saw the humility, and immediately responded by providing a new garment, shoes on his feet and a ring on his finger.

The prodigal son returning to his father parallels our coming to God the Father for His grace to save us from the penalty of sin. Grace is a concept that pervaded the Bible from beginning to end. As previous chapters have pointed out, it is based on the character of God and is demonstrated in God's dealings with man throughout history. Although God's grace is seen in all of

His dealings with mankind, it is most obvious in the salvation which He has provided. He will accept humble, repentant sinners as His own dear sons no matter what they have done. God created the world with saving grace on His mind. 1 Peter 1:18-20 tells us that the sacrifice of Christ was planned from the foundation of the world. Revelation 13:8 speaks of "The Lamb slain from the foundation of the world." So it does not surprise us to find that the very same chapter of the Bible that records the fall of man also contains the first promise of a Savior (Genesis 3:15).

The grace of God continues on through the Bible until the culmination of all things also centers on the grace of God. Ephesians 2:7 says, "That in the ages to come He might show the exceeding riches of His grace in His kindness toward us in Christ Jesus." This culmination of our salvation again involves God's dealing with mankind in grace. Revelation 21 tells us that God's ultimate goal for us, as human beings, is that He will dwell with us. This seems to express something even more than the thought of us dwelling with God. Here we have the entire divine program directed toward man and benefiting man. What a display of grace!

*Grace to you and peace from God our Father and the Lord Jesus Christ. In Him we have redemption through His blood, the forgiveness of sins, according to the riches of His grace which He made to abound toward us in all wisdom and prudence.* Ephesians 1:2,7,8

# Eighteen
# Saved by Grace Alone

*And he arose and came to his father. But when he was still a great way off, his father saw him and had compassion, and ran and fell on his neck and kissed him.* Luke 15:20

It is abundantly obvious that the prodigal had nothing to bring to the father but himself. He had squandered all that he had. All he had left was the filthy rags that he wore in the pigpen. What could he offer his father in payment for what he had wasted? Moreover, all that he had ever possessed had come from the father. So now he was not imposing on the generosity of the father, as he had earlier, but recognizing his dependence on it. He finds that the generosity of the father takes care of all that he needs.

The saving grace of God is like that; it supplies all that we need. We have nothing to bring to the heavenly Father except our sinful selves. Anything else is but filthy rags (Isaiah 64:6), for salvation is always by grace, only by grace and wholly by grace.

First of all, we must understand that salvation is always by grace. When we refer to the Dispensation of Grace we are not referring to how one is saved, for that is by grace in every dispensation. Dispensation has to do with how God deals with people and how God intervenes in the affairs of men. But eternal salvation is always based on the sacrificial death of Christ and is given as a free gift. Noah, Abraham and all the

Old Testament believers were saved by grace through faith (Genesis 6:8; 15:6).

Moreover, salvation is only by God's grace. If we add anything of man's works or human effort, it is no longer grace. Like the prodigal, we have nothing of value to bring to the father.

Salvation is wholly of grace. That is, every part of it is supplied by God's grace and we have no part in providing it. Our salvation is based on the finished work of Christ which we had no part in providing. The Holy Spirit works in our lives to convict us of sin and illuminates our minds to the truth of the gospel. The new birth is a miracle of God's grace. Living the Christian life is also by grace, as we will see in another chapter.

*For by grace you have been saved through faith, and that not of yourselves, it is the gift of God, not of works, lest anyone should boast, for we are His workmanship, created in Christ Jesus for good works, which God prepared beforehand that we should walk in them.* Ephesians 2:8−9

# Nineteen
# Living Grace

*But the father said to his servants, "Bring out the best robe and put it on him, and put a ring on his hand and sandals on his feet. And bring the fatted calf here and kill it, and let us eat and be merry; for this my son was dead and is alive again; he was lost and is found." And they began to be merry.* Luke 15:22–23

The rebellious runaway son has come back. He squandered his father's possessions, but all is forgiven. Now this generous father is even more generous. The son received gifts, but not just any kind of gift. The gifts showed that there was a new, special relationship between father and son.

"The best robe" reminds us of the robe that Jacob gave to Joseph, his favorite son. This was not work clothes. He was being honored as a favorite son.

Giving a ring involved the giving over of authority (Genesis 41:42 and Esther 3:10). A ring was often a signet ring whereby the one who had the ring in hand could conduct official business in the name of and under the authority of the king or master who gave the ring. It was a little like when we use the company's credit card today. This son now had access to the father's resources.

"Sandals on his feet" showed he was family. The servants may have been unshod. Neighborhood children playing on the grounds would have had bare feet; the family wore shoes.

We know that forgiveness is by grace, but that is only the beginning of God's work of grace. We must realize our eternal salvation involves a lot more than just being forgiven. God's saving grace puts us into a new relationship; it gives us new life and makes us new beings. Therefore, it results in a new way of living.

Some people have the notion that since God is a God of grace it does not really matter how we live. If God freely forgives, why should it concern us whether or not we sin? Does not Paul write in Romans 5:20, "But where sin abounded, grace abounded much more"? Those who talk like this do not at all understand God's grace. Paul goes on in that same part of Romans to explain that grace does more than just forgive our sins, it changes our lives. The person who says, "I'm a Christian so it does not matter how I live" probably is not a Christian because he understands neither God's grace nor His plan of salvation. How can he, therefore, ever have truly believed in Jesus? He is like a crippled man in a wheelchair who says, "I've been healed so now I can ride in a wheelchair all I want."

We are saved by grace; that is called saving grace. We also live our lives by grace. This means that the desire, strength, wisdom and ability to live the Christian life is a result of the new relationship we have with the Father through Jesus Christ and is a gift of God's grace. We might call that living grace. This living grace is what is referred to in the term "*The Dispensation of the Grace of God.*"

It is necessary for us to understand that right living is a product of God's grace. However, we ourselves are also involved in the process and need to yield to the work of grace in our lives. We do this by learning God's Word, turning from sin, and deciding to live according to our new position in Christ.

*For the grace of God that brings salvation has appeared to all men, teaching us that, denying ungodliness and worldly lusts, we should live soberly, righteously, and godly in the present age.* Titus 2:11,12

*For the Lord God is a sun and shield; the Lord will give grace and glory; no good thing will he withhold from them that walk uprightly.* Psalm 84:11

# Twenty
# Grace in Contrast

*A certain man had two sons.* Luke 15:11

There are two sons in this story. The contrast between the two sons is what makes the story interesting. The story of each son told separately would not be complete.

Therefore, we find in the Bible that the number *two* is of great significance. We know that *one* is important for God is One. We know that *three* is important for it is the number of the Godhead, the Trinity—Father, Son and Holy Spirit, three in one. *Seven* is the number of completion and rest. However, God's dealings with mankind often involve the number *two*.

1. Creation involves two totally different realms—the seen and the unseen.

2. "In the beginning God created the heavens and the earth" (Genesis 1:1).

3. God created two distinctly different kinds of human beings—male and female. "So God created man . . . male and female He created them" (Genesis 1:27). To understand God's plan for mankind, we must consider the role that God has designed for each.

4. God foretold the history of mankind to be a struggle to the death between two seeds—the seed of the woman and the seed of the serpent (Genesis 3:15).

5. There were two special trees in the Garden of Eden, the Tree of the Knowledge of Good and Evil and the Tree of Life. These can be compared to the two crosses on either side of the cross Jesus died on. One represents man's rebellion against God and involves condemnation and death. The other represents life through repentance and faith, resulting in eternal life in the paradise of God.

6. The Bible has two main parts, the Old Testament and the New Testament. The two sons in the story help us understand the contrasts between the two testaments.

There is a principle of Bible interpretation that says God sets aside the first that He might establish the second.[1] God rejected Esau and chose Jacob. Adam the first head of the race failed. God provided a second Adam in Jesus Christ. He does not fail (Romans 5:12-21). The first earth will be dissolved. The new heavens and earth will be eternal (Revelation 21:1).

Since the elder son did not appreciate or accept the generosity of the father, he did not remain in the position of honor that he should have had as the firstborn. The younger son received the blessing of the father. This was pictured in the Old Testament when father Isaac blessed Jacob instead of the firstborn brother, Esau (Genesis 27). It is fulfilled in the New Testament when God's chosen people (the nation of Israel) is set aside while gentile believers are accepted into God's household (Romans 9 and Ephesians 3:6).

This is just an introduction to these contrasts we find in the Bible, and we could go into great detail. Perhaps what will be of most help is to consider the matter of the two dispensations, which is the topic of the next chapter.

*But the free gift is not like the offense. For if by the one man's offense many died, much more the grace of God and the gift by the grace of the one Man, Jesus Christ, abounded to many.* Romans 5:15

---

[1] J. Edwin Hartill, *Principles of Biblical Hermeneutics* (Grand Rapids: Zondervan Publishing House, 1947), p. 94.

# Twenty-one
# The Dispensation of Grace—Two Sons

*So he divided to them his livelihood. And not many days after, the younger son gathered all together, journeyed to a far country, and there wasted his possession with prodigal living. Now his older son was in the field . . . . But he was angry and would not go in.* Luke 15:12,13,25,28

A generous father and two very different sons, this parallels God's dealings with mankind down through the millenniums of history[1]. The father loved them both and desired the best for them. However, both rebelled against the father's wishes. One son went out to *a far country,* away from the father's house. The other was out in the field, away from the father's house. The father had a heart of love for both of them and went out to welcome them. Yet, the circumstances were totally different because the sons were so different. So the father treated each in his own way. What was appropriate for one was not appropriate for the other.

Just as the father had to deal with his two sons very differently, God deals with mankind in two different ways. The common belief is that there are seven dispensations (innocence, conscience, human government, promise, law, grace, and kingdom [see the Appendix]). However, God treats mankind basically in one of two ways. These two different ways God deals with people alternate in the history of the human race, first one then the other, and so on. So, in a sense, there are two dispensations that alternate. At times God deals with people as a heavenly people and other times He deals with mankind as an earthly people.[2]

Adam and Eve in the Garden of Eden can be identified as an earthly people. Adam was created from the ground. The garden was created especially for them, and they were instructed to tend the garden and to keep it. Adam was given dominion over the creatures on the earth. When Adam and Eve sinned they were put out of the garden, and the way God dealt with them from then on was different.

When God deals with people as a heavenly people, His judgment is held in abeyance. Sin, for a time, goes unpunished. This is when God's grace is more evident and His holiness less evident as judgment waits. From the time that Adam and Eve were expelled from the garden until the time of Noah, sinners were not punished until the flood came. Even Cain, who killed his brother, was allowed to live a full life span. Enoch is representative of believers at that time. He was called out of the world into a closer relationship with the heavenly Father. (Genesis 5:24)

The world before the flood was like the *far country*. It was wicked and wasteful, it was enjoyable but temporary. Before the flood, Noah proclaimed righteousness (2 Peter 2:5). After the flood he was instructed to enforce righteousness (Genesis 9:5,6).[3] Before the flood, he lived among men as a stranger, knowing that all the things of this earth were but temporary. His only security was in leaving this earth by submitting to the safety of what God the Father provided. After the flood, he had authority under God, over the earth to enforce God's laws (Genesis 9:5,6).

So, we see that at times God deals with people as an earthly people. Their field of labor is the world. God gives to some responsibility and authority over peoples to carry out His will and His work in the world.[4] Their tools are laws and commandments, tabernacles and temples, divine judgment and human armies. When God deals with men as an earthly people, not only is it a time of judgment, but a time when God's people may be required to carry out this judgment.[5] In this category are Noah and his descendants during and after the flood, Moses and the Children of Israel from the ten plagues on, and the world after the church is taken out in the rapture.

When God deals with a people as heavenly people, they relate to the world as the prodigal to the *far country*. They live in the world as tourists, just passing through. Their true home is elsewhere. They have few or no ties to the country they find themselves in and are not in any position to enforce reforms in that country. God brings them out of the world as out of the *far country* and they leave it in much the same condition as it was before they came. They come into a special relationship with the Father.

Abraham and his descendants fit into this category, for "Abraham obeyed when he was called to go out to the place which he would receive as an inheritance" (Hebrews 11:8). "But now they desire a better, that is, a heavenly country. Therefore, God is not ashamed to be called their God, for He has prepared a city for them" (Hebrews 11:16). Also in this category are Enoch and his contemporaries and the church.

Moses was in a *far country* when he fled from Pharaoh to the land of Midian. But then God's way of doing things again changed—He called Moses out of the *far country*. Long overdue judgment came upon the cruel Egyptians. Moses was given authority, not only to deal with Pharaoh, but also to govern in religious and civil matters over all the children of Israel. He was given a tabernacle and rituals in order to cause the people to conform to God's requirement of worship. He was given laws and commandments to promote the standards important in people getting along as a society.

All believers today (the church) are a called-out people. The Greek word translated "church" literally means "called-out." Our home is a heavenly home (John 14:1-3), our hope is in heaven (Colossians 1:5), and our position is seated with Christ (Ephesians 2:6). Our association with the world and with our country is temporary and passing (1 Peter 2:11). Our ministry is to individuals, our weapons are spiritual (Ephesians 6: 12,13), our way of changing society is by appealing to man's conscience (2 Corinthians 4:2). So our future is that of Enoch, to walk with God (Genesis 5:24). Our present is like the life of Abraham, walking on the earth as our future inheritance, looking for a city whose builder is God (Hebrews 11:8,10).

Next on the agenda is the time of judgment described in Revelation 6-19. After that, God will again have His representatives on the earth with authority to enforce peace and righteousness.

*But God, who is rich in mercy, because of His great love with which He loved us, even when we were dead in trespasses, made us alive together with Christ (by grace you have been saved), and raised us up together, and made us sit together in the heavenly place in Christ Jesus.* Ephesians 2:4-6

[1] Most of the material in this chapter is based on the following articles: Glenn Conjurske, "The Two Dispensations," *Olde Paths and Ancient Landmarks* (November 1995), Vol. 4, No. 11, pp. 242–244.

Glenn Conjurske, "The Marrow of Dispensationalism," *Olde Paths and Ancient Landmarks* (July 1993), Vol. 2, No. 7, pp. 146–150.

[2] Glenn Conjurske, The Marrow of Dispensationalism," *Olde Paths and Ancient Landmarks* (July 1993), Vol. 2, No. 7, p. 146.

[3] Glenn Conjurske, "The Two Dispensations," *Olde Paths and Ancient Landmarks* (November 1995), Vol. 4, No. 11, p. 243.

[4] "The Marrow of Dispensationalism," p. 146.

[5] "The Two Dispensations," p. 243.

# Twenty–Two
# The Dispensation of Grace—A New Law

*So he divided to them his livelihood. And not many days after, the younger son gathered all together, journeyed to a far country, and there wasted his possession with prodigal living. Now his older son was in the field. . . . But he was angry and would not go in.* Luke 15:12,13,25,28

How does a father get his sons to stay at home and not go off to where they may never be seen again? This father used two approaches suited to the personalities of his two sons.

One approach was to give the son something to do. Keep him busy and involved. This worked to some extent with the older son. He stayed near home physically, but as far as fellowship or camaraderie between father and son, that was another matter. At times the relationship was good, but eventually it began to deteriorate until there almost was hostility between the two.

The other approach, though it was expensive and painful, worked for the younger son. He let this son leave. He gave him opportunity to experience the best and the worst of what the *far country* had to offer. The father knew that eventually the resources that the son had would be depleted and that the resources of the *far country* would not be able to satisfy him. When the son decided that home was the best place for him, the father was watching and waiting for him. Then he accepted him back like one raised from the dead. Now father and son would continually be together in heart and mind as well as physically.

In the history of mankind here on the earth, God has used various means to exercise some control over the race that He created. We refer to these systems of control as *administrations* or *dispensations*. The Dispensation of Human Government began with the institution of capital punishment in Genesis 12. The *Dispensation of Law* began with Moses when God sent plagues on Egypt and gave the Old Testament laws to the nation of Israel. Now we are under the *Dispensation of the Grace of God* (Ephesians 3:2).

Under the *Dispensation of Law* God kept His chosen people busy making sacrifices, observing feast days, and keeping laws. The tabernacle and the temple gave them access to the Father's house. However, they were so wrapped up in all the serving that most of them refused to accept the God of grace when He came and walked among them in the person of Jesus Christ.

It is the grace of God that has brought us into a new relationship with God through His Son Jesus Christ. This new relationship sets us apart from the world and gives us authority in the name of Jesus Christ. The Holy Spirit within us does the work of bringing our lives into conformity with the position that we have in Christ.

What we have under the Dispensation (or Administration) of the Grace of God is something completely new. It was never experienced in the Old Testament days. Remember it is not a new way of salvation, but a new way by which God governs in the affairs of men. This new way is characterized as never before by grace. The epistles present in detail a totally new way by which God produces right actions in the lives of His people. It is the Holy Spirit, using the truth of God's Word to produce in us the life of Christ.

*If indeed, you have heard of the dispensation of the grace of God which was given to me for you. To me, who am less than the least of all the saints, this grace was given, that I should preach among the Gentiles the unsearchable riches of Christ, and to make all see what is the fellowship* [margin dispensation] *of the mystery, which from the beginning of the ages has been hidden in God who created all things through Jesus Christ.* Ephesians 3:2,8,9

# Twenty−Three
# The Dispensation of Grace—Christ in You

*"For this my son was dead and is alive again; he was lost and is found". And they began to be merry.* Luke 15:22,23

The prodigal had come home, but would he stay home? He had rebelled, he had left home, and he had squandered his father's wealth. Now that he is back, will it start all over again? No, he has changed. He has a different attitude about himself and about his father. It was while he was herding swine that he began to see things as they really are. He came to his father with a totally different attitude. He was repentant, he was humble.

Furthermore, the father accepted him into a new relationship, more than a son—a special son with new privileges to go with his new position. It is this new, close relationship that the father wanted all along. This new relationship will keep this son from leaving home again, or it will at least bring him back if he starts to go astray.

This reminds us of the fact that our salvation involves more than just being forgiven. It involves a new relationship. If we think for a moment about what God's grace does in the process of salvation, we may recall that righteousness is credited as a result of faith. "But to him who does not work but believes on Him who justifies the ungodly, his faith is accounted for righteousness" (Romans 4:5). This means that at the moment of salvation a person has a new standing. As far as his position before God is concerned, he is righteous. His outward actions may not immediately conform to his inward standing. That is why, for example, Paul urges believers to "walk worthy of the calling with which you were called" (Ephesians 4:1). Since justification has to do with a transaction in which our sins are placed on Jesus and His righteousness is credited to our account, we still need something that works in a believer's life to cause his outward acts to conform to this inward, positional change.

This is where the word *dispensation* or *administration* comes in. What provision does God have to govern and rule in the everyday activities of individuals? The Scripture clearly indicates that this has not always been the same down through history and that the present method, if boiled down to one word, can only be described as *grace.*

What is it that governs people's lives? That governing principle in the past was law. However, the Bible says that the Christian is not under law but under grace (Romans 6: 14,15). Therefore, grace replaces law. Is it really possible to replace law—to do what law is supposed to do but cannot do? Yes! Romans 6:14,15 makes it clear that what the law could not do, God does for us by grace. So, not only are we saved by grace, but grace also governs our lives. "For the grace of God . . . has appeared . . . teaching us . . . that we should live soberly, righteously, and godly . . ." (Titus 2:11,12).

This principle by which God works in the lives of believers is best summed up in the words of Jesus in John 14:20: "You in Me, and I in you." This is what is brand-new in this administration. This is what is labeled *grace.* "To them God willed to make known what are the riches of the glory of this mystery among the Gentiles: which is Christ in you, the hope of glory" (Colossians 1:27).

*What shall we say then? Shall we continue in sin that grace may abound? Certainly not! How shall we who have died to sin live any longer in it? Or do you not know that as many of us as were baptized into Christ Jesus were baptized into His death? What then? Shall we sin because we are not under law but under grace? Certainly not!* Romans 6:1-3,15

# Twenty-Four
# Responding to Grace

*"And bring the fatted calf here and kill it, and let us eat and be merry: for this my son was dead and is alive again; he was dead and is alive again; he was lost and is found." And they began to be merry.* Luke 15:23,24

In these verses the characteristic of extreme generosity is displayed as the wayward son is welcomed home the way one would be welcomed back from the grave. However, the generous heart of the father still is not satisfied. Now there must be a response on the part of all those aware of the situation. The father has given out of a generous heart of love, but what does he desire? What does he get in return? He commands that celebration take place. He calls on his household to provide but this one thing—merriment. He expected joyful gratitude on the part of everyone involved. Now all should rejoice, what else is there to do? Any giving on the part of anyone else would only detract.

Nor is this a time to work. Joy is expressed in eating, not in working. Anyone who understands and appreciates generosity would recognize this as an extraordinary display of it and would, with thankful heart, marvel at the extent to which generosity has been shown and would find ways to demonstrate to the generous one that this display of generosity deserves to be celebrated.

The son was home, received and welcomed. The only person who would not want to rejoice and celebrate at a time like this is the person who has no understanding of generosity and no appreciation of its benefits. Unfortunately, there are individuals like this. The older brother was such a person.

When you sit down at the table to eat dinner with your family, what is the first thing you do? Probably you bow your head and "say grace." Why do we call it "saying grace" when we pray before a meal? The reason for this is that there is a connection between grace and giving thanks. In fact, in the language that the New Testament was written in, the two words are very similar. *Grace* is *charis,* and *thanksgiving* is *eucharistia.* And sometimes even the word grace *(charis)* is translated *thanks.* So you see, the same word can actually mean *grace* or *gratitude.* Gratitude is to grace like the flip side of a coin. Grace from God is generosity. Grace to God is joyful gratitude. Anything less would indicate that nothing has been received. Anything more would indicate that it was not a totally free gift. So when it comes to grace, God's part is generosity, our part is gratitude. We can evaluate ourselves and see how much we allow grace to work in our lives. Do we celebrate the generosity of God? Do we "say grace" for grace?

*Thanks be to God* [literal translation *"Grace to God"*] *for His indescribable gift!* 2 Corinthians 9:15

# Twenty-Five
# Grace and Law— The Weakness of the Law

*Now his older son was in the field. And as he came and drew near to the house, he heard music and dancing. So he called one of the servants and asked what these things meant. And he said to him, "Your brother has come, and because he has received him safe and sound, your father has killed the fatted calf." However, he was angry and would not go in. Therefore, his father came out and pleaded with him. Luke 15:25-28*

The older son was quite the opposite of his prodigal younger brother. This son stayed on the father's estate. Although he was near the father's house, he was far from the father's heart because he did not share the father's most outstanding quality. This son was not generous. He did not understand generosity nor appreciate it. He thought everything should be based on the principle of "you have to earn what you get and you get what you deserve." Therefore, he was busy in the field trying to earn the father's acceptance and approval.

Father and son got along tolerably well until the younger brother came home and the father again had occasion to show his generosity. Now the tension between the two of them came to a head. The father is more generous than ever and the older son again shows how stingy he is. Furthermore, he is jealous because his brother is enjoying the father's generosity.

The older son represents the Jews in their relationship to the Old Testament legal system. Most particularly, he is a picture of the Pharisees to whom Jesus addressed the parable (Luke 15:2,3). The Pharisees were legalists; they tried to earn favor with God by their works and law keeping. The Jews, in general, and the Pharisees, in particular, were ostensibly serving God, but they were not willing to relate to a God who shows mercy and grace on people who are totally unworthy of it. Therefore, when grace came to earth in a fuller measure, through Jesus Christ, the Jews shut themselves off from the grace of God. They were hard, legalistic and unforgiving and they thought God should be that way as well, so they rejected the God of grace.

Many of us have looked with contempt at a neighbor who has turned aside to prodigal living and has no interest in a relationship with God. But are we willing to look at our own lives and see if our relationship with God is superficial? We may be out in the field, not enjoying the Father's bounty, as far from the Father's house as the Prodigal. Unless we come to the Father with the humility of repentance, our hearts are far from Him. If we have wandered into the self-pleasing lifestyle of the *far country,* we need to humbly return to the Father's waiting arms.

However, if we are in the field of works and legalism, we need the grace of God just as desperately. The Father is pleading with us to come into His house, to leave our works and rely on His generosity. Whether we are in a *far country* or in the field refusing to enter the Father's house, His grace is available if we go to Him with humble dependence on His generosity.

*And if by grace, then it is no longer of works; otherwise, grace is no longer grace. But if it is of works, it is no longer grace; otherwise work is no longer work.* Romans 11:6

# Twenty–Six
# Grace and Law—The Purpose of the Law

*Now the older son was in the field . . . he was angry and would not go in.* Luke 15:25,28

The older son in the Parable of the Prodigal Son was out in the field. He was a worker. Now, work is a good thing and this son would be commended, except for the fact that there are some occasions when work is not good. This son refused to come in from the field at the precise time when work was not an acceptable activity. Since the brother who strayed had come home, the whole household was involved in celebration and merriment and that was the only acceptable activity at the time.

This son would not participate in the celebration because he had no appreciation for his father's generosity. Therefore, he stands in sharp contrast to his brother, who had a deep appreciation of his father's generosity.

Likewise, the grace of God stands in sharp contrast to the Old Testament system of law. Therefore, if we are to understand grace, we must see it contrasted by the law. Since the law could not do what mankind needed, grace does what the law could not do (Romans 8:3).

The law could not produce righteousness, so some aspects of the law are replaced by grace. However, the law still has a

83

function. We need to know why it was given in the first place. 1 Timothy 1:8⁻10 says that the law is for lawbreakers. Romans 3:19 says, "Now we know that whatever the law says, it says to those who are under the law, that every mouth may be stopped, and all the world may become guilty before God." That is the purpose of the law—to pronounce guilt; and this it does very well, for it has pronounced everyone in the world to be guilty. The passage goes on to say in verse 20, "for by the law is the knowledge of sin."

If you were to be involved in an automobile accident and injure your leg, when you go to the doctor, he would very likely use x⁻ray equipment. This procedure is very important in a situation like this. The thing that we want to note about the x⁻ray is that it does nothing at all for the injury. It does not set the broken bone, it does not promote healing, and it does not relieve the pain. The only purpose for the x⁻ray is to reveal the nature of the problem. This is a good illustration of the law. Just like the x⁻ray does not make anyone well, the law makes no one good. The x⁻ray is only for sick or injured people. In the same way, the law is only for bad people. As the x⁻ray shows the need for treatment, the law shows the need for the grace of God as it is made available through the gospel. Suppose the doctor were to continually use the x⁻ray machine on your leg, but never give it the attention that it needed. You would soon know that the doctor was not a real doctor but a quack. These are the kind of people Paul is upset with in 1 Timothy 1:7. These false teachers kept giving out more doses of law but never got around to talking about the cure, which is the grace of God.

*Moreover the law entered that the offense might abound. But where sin abounded, grace abounded much more, so that as sin reigned in death, even so grace might reign through righteousness to eternal life through Jesus Christ our Lord.* Romans 5:20

# Twenty-Seven
# Grace and Legalism

*So he answered and said to his father, "Lo, these many years I have been serving you; I never transgressed your commandment at any time, and yet you never gave me a young goat, that I might make merry with my friends."* Luke 15:29

The older son did not join in the celebration of his brother's return. How could he? In his mind, generosity is not a virtue. He did not understand generosity, so he could not appreciate it. His father's generosity actually made him angry. In his mind everything was, or at least should be, on the basis of good deeds and reward, work and compensatory pay. Those who do good deeds receive a reward, and those who do evil deeds must pay for what they did.

This principle of "you get what you deserve" leaves room for boasting, which this older son was quick to do. He could easily point out his worthiness by comparing himself to others, especially to his younger brother. He reminded his father of the years of diligent service he, as eldest son, had rendered. He was proud of the fact the he had always been faithful and obedient to his father. In his mind, this principle of work and reward was so important that it blinded him to what was important to the father's generous heart. He actually accused his father of being stingy, of never providing even a goat for a festive meal with his friends. However, the father insisted that all he had was his oldest son's as well. Therefore, it is obvious that the son had never asked for a goat.

The son's contempt for his father's generosity made him blind to the fact that this generosity was available to him and that he could benefit from it. He did not understand that the generosity of his father was for the benefit of those who did not deserve it but who qualified by humbly admitting that they needed it. The younger son did not qualify until he learned humility. This older son had to meet even more basic criteria. The generosity of the father was not for those who deserved it, or earned it.

One cannot show generosity by giving someone what he or she deserves. The generosity of the father was lavished on those who asked. The reason there had been no goat–roast party was that the son had never asked for one. After all, why would one want to squander even a goat (let alone a calf) on outsiders?

The actions of this older son illustrate for us what legalism is like. The Jews in Jesus' day, for the most part, were legalists. This was especially true of the Pharisees. This parable is about them and was spoken directly to them (Luke 15:2,3). The only cure for their legalism was to learn about the grace of God, because grace and legalism are contrary to each other.

It is not just the prodigal son in the *far country* who was in desperate need of the father's generosity. The older son was out in the field and would not come in to celebrate his brother's return. He could not appreciate the father's generosity toward his brother. Legalism blinded him to the value of his father's generosity. So he was left out in the field, supposedly doing the father's work, but outside the father's will, not in tune with the father's heart or enjoying the delights of the father's house.

Legalism emphasizes self–effort and glories in personal achievements. "These many years I have been serving you . . ." (Luke 15:29). Legalism is intent on the letter of the law but cannot keep the spirit of the law. "I never transgressed your commandment at any time . . ." (Luke 15:29). He may have kept the letter of the law, but the very fact that he would not celebrate shows that he was not doing the father's will. Legalism is blind to what has already been given and is intent on earning what has already been received as a gift. The son said, "You never gave me a young goat" (Luke 15:29). However, the father said, "All that I have is yours" (Luke 15:31). The son did not believe it. Legalism is trying to earn what God has already given, which is unbelief.

The story leaves the older son out in the field because there is no way to the father's heart from the father's field. The father's field represents works and legalism. The only way to the father's heart is by way of the pigpen—that is, the only way to God the Father's heart is by going through what the younger son experienced in the pigpen. Only through humble dependence on what Jesus Christ has done can we be in fellowship with the Father.

Our Father God wants us in His field serving Him. However, to do so we must first find ourselves in the Father's house partaking of His generosity. To serve Him acceptably we must understand and appreciate His grace. If we do not, our efforts at serving Him are worse than futile.

*Therefore, since we are receiving a kingdom which cannot be shaken, let us have grace, by which we may serve God acceptably with reverence and godly fear. For our God is a consuming fire.* Hebrews 12:28,29

# Twenty-Eight
# Grace Waits

*"But as soon as this son of yours came, who has devoured your livelihood with harlots; you killed the fatted calf for him." And he said to him, "Son, you are always with me, and all that I have is yours."* Luke 15:30,31

The story ends with the older son out in the field, not enjoying the celebration. He is not in the father's house and far from the father's heart. There are two reasons why the story ends this way. The other reason will be discussed in the next chapter.

The older son is left out in the field because an individual cannot gain access to the Heavenly Father's house by working in His field. All who enter the Father's house come with the humility that comes from a pigpen experience. The legalistic brother is left outside while the father pleads and waits. He is just as lost as his brother was. His brother was in a *far country* where the generosity of the father was not available. However, this older son is also in a place where he is missing out on the generosity of the father. These two individuals are sons of the father because of his part in bringing them into this world. However, the prodigal entered into a new relationship with the father when he came in humility with repentance.

All are sons of God in the sense that we owe our existence to God (1 Corinthians 8:6 and Ephesians 4:6). However, God wants us to be more than His created beings. He wants us to stop our rebelling and come to him the way the prodigal came to his father. He wants to say, "My son was dead and is alive again" (Luke 15:24).

However, we all tend to have the characteristics of the older brother to some degree or other. Perhaps most of those reading this book are more like the older son than like the younger son. So we read the Bible and try to follow the commandments of God. No matter how hard we try, it seems as if it is not enough because in the process we lose sight of grace. Our understanding of the laws of God must always be in accordance with the grace of God.

*So now, brethren, I commend you to God and to the word of His grace, which is able to build you up and give you an inheritance among all those who are sanctified.* Acts 20:32

# Twenty-Nine
# Grace for Israel

*But he was angry and would not go in. Therefore, his father came out and pleaded* [Greek "kept on pleading"] *with him.* Luke 15:28

The story leaves the older brother out in the field. However, the invitation to come join in the celebration in the father's house is left open. The father is persistent and patient. So, if the narration were continued later, how would the story end? Jesus left off telling the story with the pharisaic brother in the field because that is the situation with the nation of Israel to this day. At some future time, Israel too will join in the celebration in the Father's house.

The Pharisee, Saul of Tarsus, was the older brother and was very annoyed that God would be generous with sinners. Then he met Jesus and everything changed. Then he too welcomed the prodigal. His new attitude toward the prodigal brother, the Gentiles in the church, is stated in Ephesians 2:19, "Now, therefore, you are no longer strangers and foreigners, but fellow citizens with the saints and members of the household of God."

One day the older brother, Israel, will join us prodigal Gentiles in the big celebration in the Father's house. Then both will truly rejoice in the generosity of the Father. In that eternal celebration in the Father's house, the prodigal illustrates the bride and the older brother is the friend of the bridegroom who stands and rejoices greatly. (John 3:29, Revelation 19:6b–9.).

*Therefore, gird up the loins of your mind, be sober and rest your hope fully upon the grace that is to be brought to you at the revelation of Jesus Christ.* 1 Peter 1:13

# Thirty
# Grace Is Expressive—It Is Eternally Displayed

*And he said to him, "Son, you are always with me, and all that I have is yours."* Luke 15:31

The father in the parable shows his generosity repeatedly, but at the end of the story, there are several clues that show the story could continue, with more of the father's generosity to be experienced in the future. The Prodigal has returned to the father's house and heart and has a new, closer relationship with the father than he ever had before. The father kept on pleading with the older son to enjoy the generosity available to him. The promise "all that I have is yours" is yet to be fully experienced by the sons.

We hear and read about the marvelous grace of God and sometimes wonder if His grace really is all that fantastic. Why do we not see more obvious displays of His generosity? Could not His grace do away with sickness and pain? Why do we have just barely enough money to pay the bills? Why do we not have instant answers to all our prayer? We wonder if God's grace is really that amazing after all. Yes, the grace of God is even more wonderful than we can imagine; however, the full revealing of it is still in the future.

The greatest display of God's grace is yet to be seen. In God's plan for mankind there is yet a future time coming when we will experience God's grace to the fullest extent. Two verses in particular point this out. Ephesians 2:7 says, "that in the ages to come He might show the exceeding riches of His grace in His kindness toward us in Christ Jesus." The grace of God will be put on display in ages to come. For now, it is not so obvious. 1 Peter 1:13 also tells us about this future aspect of grace. "Therefore, gird up the loins of your mind, be sober, and rest your hope fully upon the grace that is to be brought to you at the revelation of Jesus Christ."

This future display will last forever (Romans 5:21). It will provide continuous pleasure (Psalm 16:11). All sadness will be eliminated (Revelation 21:4). God's grace involves an eternal personal relationship with Him—serving Him, worshiping Him, fellowshipping with Him (Revelation 21:3).

*But God, who is rich in mercy, because of His great love with which He loved us, even when we were dead in trespasses, made us alive together with Christ (by grace you have been saved), and raised us up together, and made us sit together in the heavenly places in Christ Jesus, that in the ages to come He might show the exceeding riches of His grace in His kindness toward us in Christ Jesus.* Ephesians 2:4–7

# Thirty-One
# Grace Rejected

*So he answered and said to his father, "Lo, these many years I have been serving you; I never transgressed your commandment at any time, and yet you never gave me a young goat, that I might make merry with my friends. However, as soon as this son of yours came, who has devoured your livelihood with harlots, you killed the fatted calf for him." And he said to him, "Son, you are always with me, and all that I have is yours."* Luke 15:30,31

The two young men are brothers, yet in some ways they are totally different. The younger of the two misused the father's generosity. The older brother refused the father's generosity. The younger son is the black sheep of the family. The older one seemed to be the ideal son. He served the father faithfully, while the other son took all the money he could get his hands on and left. The older son obeyed the father in the letter of the law; however, his heart was not in it. He did not accept or agree with that which was the father's greatest joy.

Physically he was in the father's field but morally he was in the *far country*. His body did not go to the *far country* but his mind did. He accused his brother of spending the father's wealth on prostitutes, not because he knew what his brother had done but because he knew what he would do. The only reason he was not out in the *far country* was he was too proud. His faithfulness to the father was merely for show. His work for the father was just for the sake of appearances.

The father's greatest joy was in giving, and in giving generously. The older brother did not enjoy giving or receiving. He accused his father of being unwilling to provide even a goat for a feast with his friends. However, the reason he did not have a goat for celebrating with his friends was because he did not ask. He did not ask because he was too selfish to throw a party for his friends.

The younger son was on the receiving end of the father's generosity. However, the older brother refused to accept his inheritance. It seems unlikely that any one would respond this way toward a generous father, however, most of us are prone to respond that way toward a generous God.

The older brother represents what many of us are: proud, self-righteous, legalistic and lacking in faith. We do not participate in worldly things because we would be embarrassed to be seen doing those things, not because spiritual things have a priority in our lives. We like to compare ourselves with others instead of following Jesus as our example. We expect God to appreciate what we do and to condemn those who do not measure up to our standards. When others receive favors from God that we neither received nor even expected to receive, we are jealous and blame God. This was the attitude of the Pharisees who constantly opposed Jesus during His years of earthly ministry. Jesus severely renounced them. Likewise, we cannot expect to become true followers of Jesus with this kind of attitude. The way to the home and heart of the Father is learned in a *pigpen* experience. No wonder that the publicans and prostitutes were more likely to become followers of Jesus than the Pharisees were.

If life has dealt you *pigpen* circumstances, accept them with gratitude because only humility such as learned in the *pigpen* will allow us to experience to the fullest the abundant grace of God.

*God resists the proud, but gives grace to the humble. Therefore, humble yourselves under the mighty hand of God, that He may exalt you in due time.* 1 Peter 5:5,6

# Thirty-Two
# Grace Vindicated

*It was right that we should make merry and be glad, for your brother was dead and is alive again, and was lost and is found.*
Luke 15:32

The father's one outstanding quality is that he is generous. Whatever else he may do, he must be true and faithful to himself and act accordingly. By not coming in from the field, the older son challenged his father's actions. He accused him of being unfair. He thought the father was wrong in being so generous towards the prodigal brother. Therefore, the father must defend his actions and his character. The father gives assurance that all that he does is right. There is physical evidence of this. The lost brother is found; the son who was gone, as good as dead, is now alive. This one life saved makes it all right and good. The son, safe at home with the father, is all the vindication that the father needed for all of his acts of generosity.

Our God, the Heavenly Father, likewise, vindicates His generosity. The price that He paid to make His grace available to us was the death of His Son. Some might question whether it was proper for God to deliberately let His Son suffer and die in our place. However, the Bible tells us that it was a fitting thing to do, for in this He brings us into an eternal relationship with Himself. "For it was fitting for Him, for whom are all things and by whom are all things, in bringing many sons to glory, to make the captain of their salvation perfect through sufferings" (Hebrews 2:10). If God needs any physical evidence to show that He was right in His generosity toward mankind at the expense of His Son, we are that evidence. Our eternal presence in His house makes all that He does right and worthwhile. It is proper and appropriate that we should celebrate and rejoice in our salvation, even though it involves such an awful sacrifice, for by that sacrifice the marvelous grace of God is made possible.

*But God forbid that I should boast except in the cross of our Lord Jesus Christ, by whom the world is crucified to me and I to the world.* Galatians 6:14

# Thirty-Three
# Grace for Today and Forever

*And bring the fatted calf here and kill it, and let us eat and be merry. Now the older son was in the field. Therefore, his father came out and pleaded with him.* Luke 15:23,25,28

How does the story end? When we read an interesting story, we are always wondering how it will end. Will it have a happy ending or a tearful ending? Will they "live happily ever after"? In the story that Jesus told about a generous father and his two sons, we do well to note where the story leaves the main characters.

The younger son, the one who went astray and squandered the father's wealth, is in the father's house. He is enjoying activities, relationships, possessions and opportunities he never dreamed would be his. That is the end of the story as far as he is concerned.

What a picture of God's grace as His children will enjoy it for all eternity. There will be endless celebration with the Heavenly Father. There will be no looking at our own goodness, only rejoicing in the generosity of God. No reminders of how low we fell. The stench of the pigpen is forgotten. The filthy rags are far removed.

This is what God has in store for those who humbly come to him, recognizing their dependence on His grace.

The older son, because of his pride, is out in the field, not enjoying the generosity of the father. He does not enjoy the bounties of the father's house. However, the father is still out in the field patiently pleading with him, waiting for him as he had waited for the prodigal son.

*The Dispensation of the Grace of God* involves God's patient forbearance. The grace of God withholds judgment so that He can show His grace while He waits and pleads with individuals to respond to His gracious invitation to join Him in an eternal celebration in the Father's house.

*Being justified freely by His grace through the redemption that is in Christ Jesus.* Romans 3:24

# Appendix A
# Short Explanation of Dispensationalism

In the original language of the New Testament, the word that in our English Bible is translated *dispensation* or *administration* is made up of two words, *house* and *law*. A dispensation is how God governs His household. A closely related word is *steward*, which refers to an individual who manages a household.

Does God change His house laws from time to time? The fact that He has changed them is obvious if you have read enough of the Bible to notice the contrast between the Old Testament and the New Testament. Therefore, we have at least two dispensations. Most dispensational teaching presents seven dispensations. Those who reject a dispensational approach to understanding the Bible minimize the differences between the Old and New Testament. In doing this they interpret some passages figuratively where the dispensationalist takes the Bible literally.

A dispensational approach to understanding the Bible is valid and important. However, there are some errors that are common and dangers that are present in the way dispensations are often presented. Most of these problems have to do with grace. Dispensational teaching often gives the impression that today we are saved by grace but in other dispensations salvation was not by grace. This is not true; salvation has always been by grace through faith. If the dispensation of grace does not refer to the fact that we are saved by grace, why is it described as "of grace"? It is the dispensation of grace because godly living is by grace in a way that it never was under other dispensations. In other words, the house laws are characterized by grace as never before.

Therefore, this study of grace emphasizes both grace as it relates to godly living and grace as it relates to God's dealings with mankind throughout history and in the future.

*The grace of the Lord Jesus Christ, and the love of God, and the communion of the Holy Spirit be with you all. Amen.*
2 Corinthians 13:14

# Appendix B
# Presentation of a Dispensational System

This book on the grace of God comes out of a study of the Bible from a dispensational approach that is somewhat different from how it is usually taught. This appendix examines the advantages of a dispensational approach and some of the errors that have come with it. It then presents a dispensational system that the author believes is Biblical and is extremely helpful in understanding the Bible and how the contrasts between the Old Testament and the New Testament can be reconciled.

Old Testament believers were promised blessings if they obeyed (Deuteronomy 28) and New Testament believers are told that they have been blessed "with every spiritual blessing" (Ephesians 1:3). Saul was told to destroy and put to death the entire nation of Amalek (1 Samuel 15:3). In the New Testament we are told to love our enemies (Matthew 5:44) and that warfare is to be only in the spiritual realm (Ephesians 6:12). This study of grace and dispensations is presented to help in understanding these differences.

The word *dispensation* seems to have fallen into disrepute in recent years. There are several reasons for this. The first reason is that the word itself does not really communicate well the theology that it represents. We get the word from the Authorized King James Bible, but it is not a word that the average person on the street would fully understand. We need to carefully define the word, if not replace it.

Secondly, dispensational theology is based on a literal interpretation of the Bible. It is based on the premise that though the Bible seems to present conflicting theology, it actually means what it says, and still somehow it all fits together. The modem trend in theology, on the other hand, is to accept those parts of the Bible that are most acceptable, and to reject or reinterpret those parts that do not fit.

The third reason why dispensational theology is becoming unpopular is that it is often misrepresented and misunderstood. Too often dispensationalism is taught in isolation from other important Bible teachings so that it appears to be little more than history chopped into seven periods of time, and events arranged into an artificially parallel pattern.

Most presentations of dispensations are centered on a description of seven periods of time in the chronology of God's dealings with mankind. This kind of presentation is inadequate, for it leaves out some basic considerations. This book was written to deal with these neglected topics. There may be some individuals, who, after reading this far, are interested in studying dispensationalism as a system of theology as it relates to matters other than the grace of God. It is for these individuals that this appendix is included.

The first part of this appendix will give a description of dispensationalism and deals with the four doctrines that are basic to it. The second part presents a dispensational system that is in alignment with the truths presented in the chapters of this book.

**What Dispensationalism Is**


Dispensationalism is a rather simple idea that often has wrapped around it a very complex system. This simple idea must be clearly understood, although one may not fully understand the complete system.


**Dispensationalism Is Recognizing Distinctions**


At the root of dispensationalism is an emphasis on recognizing distinction in the Bible.[1] Recognizing distinctions where they occur is one of the basic principles of Bible interpretation.[2]


Every Bible interpreter recognizes distinctions in the Bible.[3] For example, everyone recognizes that there is both the New Testament and the Old Testament. There is a difference between law and grace, between faith and works, between physical blessings and spiritual blessings, between Sabbath keeping and first day gatherings, etc. In a sense, everyone "who trusts the blood of Christ rather than bringing an animal sacrifice" is a dispensationalist.[4]


Although all interpreters recognize these differences, not all consider themselves to be dispensationalists. The non-dispensationalist sees these differences as so obvious that no system is needed to explain them. He emphasizes a unifying principle that will tie all things together.[5] The dispensationalist, on the other hand, sees these differences as so great that he has developed a system of theology whereby he can understand, systematize, and explain them.

Against this theological system the non-dispensationalist takes his stand. It is a system that he considers unnecessary and heretical. He thinks it splinters the unity of the Bible.

## Dispensationalism Is a System of Hermeneutics

A detailed study of the dispensational system is difficult for two reasons. First, it has grown into a complicated system that affects both the interpretation of very many passages of Scripture and also of one's understanding of most areas of theology. Secondly, there are many variations of the dispensational system. Each dispensational scholar has a somewhat different approach or emphasis in his dispensational system. However, there are at least four doctrines that set dispensational interpreters apart from other Bible scholars.

## Literal Interpretation

One of the basic emphases of dispensationalism is that "it applies the literal rule of interpretation to the whole Bible."[6] This grammatical–historical method of interpretation is insisted upon for interpreting both the Old Testament and the New Testament; both for interpreting history and for interpreting prophecy. The dispensationalist recognizes that there are many figures of speech in the Scripture, but resorts to non–literal interpretation only when the figure of speech is obvious or when the literal expression cannot make sense at all.

## Premillennial Eschatology

It is beyond the scope of this book to go into detail in the area of prophecy, but it should be noted that premillennialism has always been a part of the dispensational approach to Scripture and has been propagated primarily by dispensational teachers.[7] The dispensationalist's emphasis on recognizing distinctions and on literal interpretation naturally brings him to this eschatological position. He cannot conceive of a kingdom, such as described in the prophetic Scripture, existing on the earth without the literal, physical presence of the Son of David, sitting on the throne of David as the Scriptures prophesied.

## Church/Israel Distinction

A dispensationalist keeps Israel and the church distinct.[8] This distinction is at the heart of dispensationalism. It provides the basis for distinguishing the manner in which God deals with individuals today from the way He dealt with individuals in Old Testament times and from the manner in which He will deal with men in the future. It provides the pattern for all of the dispensational distinctions which are recognized by the dispensationalist.

## Progressive Revelation

Another matter that must be considered is the progressive nature of God's revelation to man.[9] Progressive revelation is clearly indicated in Scripture, for example, Hebrews 1:1,2. "God, who at various times and in various ways spoke in time past to the fathers by the prophets, has in these last days spoken to us by His Son . . . ."

God did not reveal all truth at one time. God revealed some truth to Adam. He revealed additional truth to the Patriarchs. The prophets received additional revelation. Revelation climaxed in Jesus Christ and His Apostles. Recognizing this progression of Revelation influences how one understands basic Bible doctrine.

Dispensationalists are accused of dividing up the Scriptures so that most of it has no primary application to believers today.[10] Here again, the progressive nature in which God revealed truth to man must be taken into account. Progressive revelation does not mean that God changes or that His standards change. Any Scripture that deals with this aspect of revelation, therefore, is equally valid to all generations.

However, as additional revelation is given, God provided not only additional responsibility in light of additional enlightenment, but He also provides additional enablement to meet that responsibility. Therefore, "All Scripture is . . . profitable for doctrine, for reproof, for connection, for instruction in righteousness" (2 Timothy 3:16). This is true because Scripture tells man about God's character and standards, and these never change.

**Alternating Dispensations**

The biggest benefit that dispensationalism offers to the Bible student is that it helps one to understand the Scriptures. This tremendous help in understanding the Bible does not come primarily from a knowledge of the various tests, judgments, and failures (on man's part) that are sometimes presented as the main features of the various dispensations. The benefit comes from seeing the general framework of God's dealing with mankind throughout history. This understanding of an overall pattern becomes a hermeneutical tool helpful in grasping the revealed truth as it was given in progressive stages.[11]

According to Kurtaneck, "progressive revelation accounts for the variety and diversity in God's dealings with man throughout history."[12] A review of chapters 21, 22 and 23 will remind the reader that the variety and the diversity in God's dealing with man is not just because of the progressive nature of His revelation, but is a demonstration of the two sides of His character and that God, in His dealings with man, alternates between forbearance and judgment.

This alternating between what are essentially only two dispensations is a phenomenon that very few Bible scholars have taken note of. Therefore, they err in trying to explain the changes in the way God deals with mankind by only pointing to the fact of progressive revelation. The understanding of dispensations as presented in chapters 21, 22 and 23 goes much further in explaining the differences and seeming contradictions in the Bible than does the progressive revelation principle.

## Understanding Dispensations

If by dispensation we mean all of God's dealings with man, and salvation is part of the dealing, then a new dispensation indicates a different way of salvation. Since we believe there is only one way of salvation, then we have to have a narrower definition of dispensation.

When it comes to eternal salvation, God's method is changeless. "Since no other freedom to act in behalf of sinners has been secured, it is to be concluded that all God has done or will do for sinful men is wrought on the sole basis of Christ's death."[13] There are other aspects of God's dealings with men that also do not change from one dispensation to another. Therefore, a narrower definition of dispensation is in order. I would suggest the following: a dispensation is the rule of life that God has given to govern a particular group of people.

Taking this definition as a basis, two steps are involved in setting up a dispensational system. First, one needs to identify the groups of people involved in God's dealings with mankind. Secondly, the contrast between the governing principles needs to be noted.

## Identify the Groups

In the process of God's dealing with mankind from eternity past to eternity future, six groups of people can be distinguished.

### Adam and Eve Before the Fall

Before Adam and Eve committed their first sin, God was able to deal with them in unique ways, in ways that were not possible after the fall, nor are possible now (Genesis 2:15–3:24).

### Adam and His Descendants After the Fall

After the fall of man into sin, God's dealing with mankind changed, but it applied equally to the whole human race and was consistent and fair.

## Noah and His Descendants

The universal flood destroyed almost all the descendants of Adam and Eve. Noah and his family received special grace from God. Therefore, the group that God dealt with after the flood, though it included all the inhabitants of the earth, was limited to Noah and his descendants.

## Abraham and His Descendants

After the confusion of languages at the Tower of Babel, God no longer dealt with the human race as a whole, but chose one particular family with which He might enter into a covenant relationship.[14] So, we find from Genesis 12 through the rest of the Old Testament, very little is said about mankind as a whole, but much attention is given to Abraham and his descendants.

Romans 9:4,5 points out what was God's way of dealing with them in contrast to the rest of the world. "Who are Israelites, to whom pertain the adoption, the glory, the covenants, the giving of the law, the services of God, and the promises; of whom are the fathers and from whom, according to the flesh, Christ came, who is over all the eternally blessed God. Amen." Those who were not a part of this group are described as "strangers from the covenants of promise, having no hope and without God in the world" (Ephesians 2:12).

## The Church

Beginning at Pentecost, God formed and began dealing with a new group of people. This group is made up of both Jews and Gentiles (Ephesians 2:13,14; 3:6). This allowed all peoples of the world the opportunity to be a part of God's household.

"For through Him we both have access by one Spirit to the Father. Now, therefore, you are no longer strangers and foreigners, but fellow citizens, with the saints, and members of the household of God" (Ephesians 2:18,19).

## The Millennial Kingdom

The final group of people that needs to be identified is the inhabitants of the millennial kingdom. Again, both Jews and Gentiles are involved (Isaiah 62:2). In fact, all the people then on this earth will be under the direct rule of Christ (Revelation 10:15).

## Identify the Ruling Principle

Having identified distinct groups of people with whom God has specific dealings, it is necessary to determine whether there is a difference in the way God deals with them and what these differences are. As has already been noted, the difference is not in how people are saved but in how God governs their lives. Kurtaneck states the matter as follows: "The fact of the matter is that both law and grace, as faith and works, have existed in each economy in some form since Adam's fall. However, law and grace did not exist in every dispensation as a rule of life."[15]

The precise principle by which God rules a particular group is not always easy to determine. However, the Bible deals at length with at least three distinct governing principles. Therefore, though one cannot be precise about every distinct ruling of God, the Bible is quite clear about some of them. It might be well to begin with the ones that are most clear.

## The Mosaic Law

From the time that it was given at Mount Sinai until it was terminated at the cross (Colossians 2:14), the Law of Moses served as the rule of life for God's people.[16] "The Bible never confuses grace and law as to their respective positions in the progressive revelation of the divine plan. As rules of life, they are distinct . . . ."[17] The Law of Moses was powerless to save people from sin (Romans 8:2–4), but it was a complete and righteous rule of life. "Therefore, the law is holy, and the commandment holy and just and good" (Romans 7:12).

## The Literal Physical Presence of the King

Though the millennial kingdom will involve the ruling activity of believers (Revelation 20:4), the throne of David (Ezekiel 27:24; 34:23,24), and laws written in the hearts of individuals (Jeremiah 31:33), yet it is clear that the key ruling principle will involve the physical presence of the King of Kings. His presence will bring righteousness and equity (Isaiah 11:4). "These great moral principles of the mediatorial government will be enforced by sanctions of supernatural power."[18] The symbol of this power is the rod of iron (Isaiah 11:4, Revelation 19:15).

## Human Government

Human government as a ruling principle was ordained by God (Romans 13:1,2). The authority for the exercise of human government was given to Noah as recorded in Genesis 9:5,6. It is important to notice that this ruling principle is still in effect today,[19] as is clear from the Romans 13 passage. When God began to deal with only one particular family (Abraham and his descendants), He did not leave the rest of the world without a ruling principle. Although "it is true that Satan holds the world governments in control (cf. Matthew 4:8,9, Luke 4:5-7), and that they are exercised under Gentile authority throughout this age . . .",[20] yet human government remains as God's ordained authority over the world (Romans 13:1,2) and God is still in ultimate control of all things.

**Other Ruling Principles**

The Law of Moses, as a rule of life, involves most of the Old Testament history. Only Genesis and the first part of Exodus cover time when people were not under the Mosaic Law.[21] Other principles were in effect governing individuals' lives. These principles are not as clearly stated and developed as later ones. From the fall to the flood, the governing principle might be said to be the heart of man (Genesis 6:5). It is even harder to be precise about the life-governing principles in effect before the fall. Most call it innocence.[22] It is the opinion of this writer that Adam and Eve, before the fall, were governed (in moral matters) by something like intuition or instinct.

However, to be dogmatic about these other ruling principles leads one into the kind of errors that were mentioned earlier in this section.

**The Grace of God**

How does God govern the lives of His people today? The present dispensation is called the dispensation of the grace of God. Is this a valid way to designate the governing principle? Yes, though the word "grace" is more often associated with our salvation; in this dispensation there is not only saving grace, but also grace for godly living.

A supernatural power is provided for the exact and perfect execution of the superhuman rule of life under grace. There is no aspect of the teaching of grace which is more vital than this, or which so fully differentiates these teachings from every other rule of life in the Bible. Under grace, all‑powerful, abiding, indwelling, and sufficient Holy Spirit of God is given to every saved person.[23]

The unique aspect of this dispensation is not how people get saved, but that godly living is by grace. This is not to say that Old Testament believers did not have divine enablement for living. For the New Testament believer, godly living is accomplished by an entirely new principle.

For example, the motivation for godly living is different. For the Israelites the motivation was, "if you diligently obey the voice of the LORD your God, to observe carefully all His commandments which I command you today . . . all these blessings shall come upon you . . ." (Deuteronomy 28:1‑3). For the New Testament believer the motivation is, "for the love of Christ compels us" (2 Corinthians 5:14). This rule of grace comes to the believer in the person of the Holy Spirit. Many New Testament passages make this clear. For example, Galatians 5:18 says, "But if you are led by the Spirit, you are not under the law."

"It is the supreme purpose of the Spirit to reproduce Christ‑likeness in the believer."[24] This is made clear in Romans 8:29 and 2 Corinthians 3:16. This principle is also described as the life of Christ within the believer. In Galatians 4:19, Paul, writing to believers, says, "My little children, for whom I labor in birth again until Christ is formed in you."

This discussion of grace for living could go on almost indefinitely. Therefore, this is the one aspect of Dispensationalism that should be the central theme of most preaching. It certainly is the central theme of most of Paul's writings.

## Conclusions

Dispensationalism is a valid area of study. It not only recognizes distinctions in the Bible, but also seeks to understand them based on changes in God's dealing with His people. These changes find their basis in the manifold characteristics and attributes of God in conjunction with the truth of progressive revelation. Much that one finds in a dispensational system points to the fact that more careful Bible study must be done in this area so that a truly biblical approach may be achieved.

It is the conclusion of this writer that such an approach would be more acceptable to those whose backgrounds are not in Dispensationalism and would help them to understand the contrast between the Old Testament and the New Testament. A Biblical approach to Dispensationalism also helps the believer to understand the grace that God provides for Christian living as it stands in contrast to the legal system of the Old Testament.

All of us have formulated ideas of how the Bible is to be understood and how it fits together. The easiest thing for us to do is to find Scripture passages that uphold our original position and stick to it. However, when studying the Bible, the virtuous thing is not necessarily to stick with one's own opinion, but to know what the Bible teaches and to constantly strive to understand it better.

[1]  Charles Caldwell Ryrie, *Dispensationalism Today* (Chicago: Moody Press, 1965), p. 15.

[2]  J. Edwin Hartill, *Principles of Biblical Hermeneutics* (Grand Rapids: Zondervan Publishing House, 1947), p. 20.

[3]  Ryrie, p. 16.

[4]  Lewis Sperry Chafer, *Dispensationalism* (Reprinted from "Bibliotheca Sacra" Number 372, Vol. 93, Oct. –Dec. 1936, Dallas: Dallas Theological Seminary, 1936, p. 391.

[5]  Ryrie. p. 18.

[6]  Nickolas Kurtaneck, "Dispensationalism—A Builder of Faith" (Unpublished manuscript of Bauman Memorial Lectures, Winona Lake: Grace Theological Seminary, 1977), ch. 1. p. 39.

[7]  Robert G. Clouse, *The Meaning of the Millennium* (Downers Grove: InterVarsity Press, 1977), p. 12.

[8]  Ryrie, p. 44.

[9]  Kurtaneck, ch. 1, p. 46.

[10]  Clarence B. Bass, *Backgrounds to Dispensationalism* (Grand Rapids: Baker Book House, 1960), pp. 37–38.

[11]  Frank E. Gaebelein, Forward to *Dispensationalism Today* (Chicago: Moody Press, 1965), p. 8.

[12]  Ibid.

13  Chafer, *Dispensationalism,* p. 427.

14  R. I. Humberd, *The Dispensations* (Flora. IN: R. I. Humberd Christian Book depot. n.d), p. 31.

15  Kurtaneck, ch. 2, p. 10.

16  Ibid, p. 32.

17  Ibid.

18  Alva J. McClain, *The Greatness of the Kingdom* (Grand Rapids: Zondervan Publishing House, 1959), p. 208.

19  Chafer, *Major Bible Themes,* p. 131.

20  Lewis Sperry Chafer, *Systematic Theology* (Dallas: Dallas Seminary Press, 1947, 1948), Vol. IV. p. 196.

21  Kurtaneck, ch. 2, p. 32.

22  Scofield, p. 5; Chafer, *Major Bible Themes,* p. 129.

23  Chafer, *Systematic Theology,* Vol. IV. pp. 188–189.

24  Ibid., p. 193.

# Appendix C
# Dispensational Charts
God's Dealings with Men Throughout History

## Notes on the Chart

The chart is adapted from an unpublished chart by the late Glenn Conjurske.

The purpose of this chart is to help one to visualize the ideas presented in this book. The Scripture passages listed in it explain the various aspects of it.

Note the following characteristics of the chart:

>The emphasis is not on the dispensations as such, but on the groups of people to which they pertain.

>The seven dispensations of Scofield and others line up with the elements of this chart but are not the central emphasis of it. The dispensations alternate between forbearance and judgment. When God deals with mankind with forbearance, judgment is delayed; God's people are dealt with as a heavenly people.

>Enoch and Abraham are Old Testament representatives of how God deals with the righteous. Believers today are in a

category with them. The rest of the world is allowed to continue in their sin until the time of judgment.

>Following each of the dispensations of forbearance comes judgment and then a time when righteousness is enforced. Noah, after the flood, and Moses, after deliverance from Egypt, were God's representatives to enforce righteousness on the earth. This sets the pattern for the coming of Christ, when righteousness will be enforced throughout the whole world.

>In one case, the group that God has dealt with ceases to exist as such, thus ending the dispensation. Other times, the group continues to exist but God chooses a new group with which He deals in a particular way. The old group then continues under the dispensation of human government.

>This chart points out that when God dealt with Israel in a particular way, God's house laws pertained only to that nation, but the rest of the world was still under the dispensation of human government.

>Likewise, God's house laws today pertain to the church and not to the world as a whole.

>A distinction is made between dispensation and age.

>The church is not judged by destruction or abandonment but is taken from the scene.

>The future dispensation as such does not start until after the judgment of nations, but the lives of some of the people who will be in it will have already begun before that time.

# GOD'S DEALING WITH MEN THROUGHOUT HISTORY

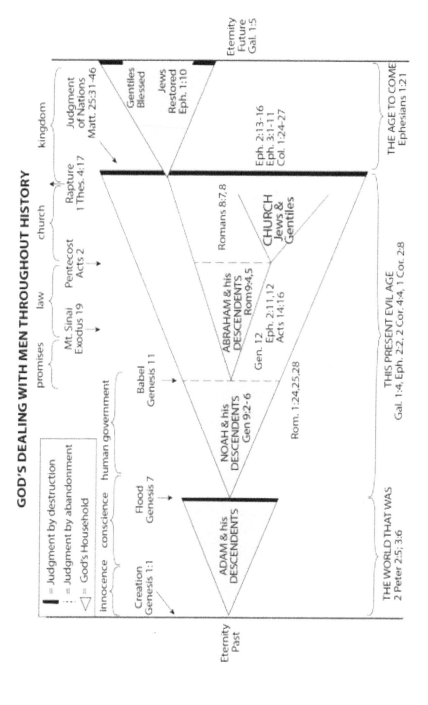

= Judgment by destruction

= Judgment by abandonment

= God's Household

innocence   conscience   human government

promises   law   church   kingdom

Creation
Genesis 1:1

Flood
Genesis 7

Babel
Genesis 11

Mt. Sinai
Exodus 19

Pentecost
Acts 2

Rapture
1 Thes. 4:17

Judgment
of Nations
Matt. 25:31-46

Gentiles
Blessed

Jews
Restored
Eph. 1:10

Eternity
Future
Gal. 1:5

Eternity
Past

ADAM & his
DESCENDENTS

NOAH & his
DESCENDENTS
Gen 9:2-6

ABRAHAM & his
DESCENDENTS
Rom 9:4,5

Gen. 12
Eph. 2:11,12
Acts 14:16

CHURCH
Jews &
Gentiles

Rom. 1:24,25,28

Romans 8:7,8

Eph. 2:13-16
Eph. 3:1-11
Col. 1:24-27

THE WORLD THAT WAS
2 Peter 2:5; 3:6

THIS PRESENT EVIL AGE
Gal. 1:4, Eph. 2:2, 2 Cor. 4:4, 1 Cor. 2:8

THE AGE TO COME
Ephesians 1:21

125

## Seven Dispensations[1] Charted

| | Innocence | Conscience | Government | Promise | Law | Grace | Kingdom |
|---|---|---|---|---|---|---|---|
| Characteristic of God's People | Earthly | Heavenly | Earthly | Heavenly | Earthly | Heavenly | Earthly |
| Beginning Event | Creation | Abel's sacrifice accepted | World wide flood | Call of Abraham | Plagues of Egypt | Pentecost | Judgments of Revelation |
| Representative | Adam | Enoch | Noah | Abraham | Moses | Every Believer | Overcomer Rev 3:5 |
| Authority over sin | Command of God | Forebearance[2] | Human Government | Forebearance[2] | Mosaic Law | Forebearance[2] | Rod of iron Rev. 2:27, 19:5 |
| Provision for Righteousness | Obey or die Gen 2:17 | By faith offer a sacrifice & walk with God Heb 11:4,5 & Gen. 5:24 | Obey those in authority Gen 9:5,6 Rom 13:1-7 | Faith credited for righteousness Rom. 4:3 | Obey & be blessed, disobey & be cursed Deut. 28 | Christ in you, the hope of glory Col. 1:27 | Obey or feel the rod Isaiah 65:20 |
| God's People | In charge of the world Gen 1:26 | Taken to heaven Gen. 5:24 | Represent God's authority on earth Gen 9:5 | Live as strangers on the earth Heb. 11:8-16 | Function as prophets, priests, and kings | Share the gospel Matt. 28:19,20 | Reign with Christ Rev 20:4 |
| Household | Adam & Eve | Adam & descendants | Noah & descendants | Abraham & descendants | Nation of Israel | Church | Sheep (Judgment of Nations) Matt 25:34 |
| House Law[1] | Don't eat the forbidden fruit Gen. 2:17 | Do what is right Gen. 6:5 | Obey those in authority Gen. 9:5,6 Rom. 13:1-7 | Believe the promises Gen. 15:6 | Obey & be blessed, disobey & be cursed Deut. 28 | Be led by the indwelling Spirit Rom. 8:14 | Submit to the literal presence of God Rev 2:27 |
| Ending Event | Man falls into sin | Ark of safety closed | Scattering at Babel[3] | Deliverance from Egypt | Christ crucified[3] | Rapture | Merges into eternity |
| Age | The world that was 2 Peter 2:5, 3:6 | | | This present evil age Gal. 1:4, 2 Cor. 4:4 | | | Ages to come Eph. 2:7 |

[1] Dispensation in the Greek is oikonomia which is literally "house law."

[2] Forebearance means that judgment is delayed. Sinners are allowed to go their own way.

[3] Human government has not ceased but continues to function until Jesus Christ takes control.
However, a new dispensation begins as God chooses one family that He deals with.
Also, God's dealing with Israel under law will resume for Daniel's 70th week (Matthew 24:20).

Made in the USA
Las Vegas, NV
05 April 2022

46897193R00075